The Coming Temple

The Coming Temple:

Center Stage
For The Final Countdown

By

Don Stewart and Chuck Missler

The Coming Temple

Published by Dart Press
Box 6486
Orange, California 92613

ISBN 1-877825-07-7

Library of Congress Catalogue Card Number 91-71881

PRINTED IN THE UNITED STATES OF AMERICA

Scripture quotations are used from The Holy Bible, New King James Bible, © 1979, 1980, 1982 by Thomas Nelson Inc. Nashville, Tennessee and are used by permission.

Second Printing January 1992

To our wonderful friends in Israel

this book is lovingly dedicated.

TABLE OF CONTENTS

INTRODUCTION

The subject of a future Temple in Jerusalem is the cause of much controversy among Jews, Christians, and Moslems. Will a Third Temple be built? If so, what will happen to the Dome of the Rock and the Al Aqsa Mosque? What does the Third Temple have do with the coming of the Messiah? Why are evangelical Christians so interested in events surrounding the Temple Mount?

These questions, along with many others are on the minds of millions of Jews, Christians, and Moslems. The Temple Mount is the target area where these three faiths clash. This being the case, a book about the Temple Mount is in order.

The authors feel they are in a unique position to write about this subject. In the past ten years, we have had the privilege to become friends with some of the personalities in Israel who are involved in various movements to initiate the building of a Third Temple. We also have been part of a scientific expedition that attempted to locate the exact site of where the First and Second Temple stood. As veteran Bible teachers, we are also familiar with what the Scripture has to say concerning the subject of a future Temple.

Scope

This book is not meant to be an exhaustive, technical treatise. The authors are painfully aware that much more space could be given to many of the subjects they treat. We have added footnotes, appendices, as well as a bibliography for those who wish to do further work on their own. It is our plan to do future works on related subjects.

Some of the possibilities presented are little more than informed conjectures which await additional evidence for confirmation or amendment. Scholarly inquiry and the technology of the 90's will quickly make obsolete some of the views included in our brief work. We plan to keep this work up to date with frequent revisons as new discoveries warrant. Further scientific expeditions are also planned.

Our primary interest is to acquaint our readers with the incredible adventure that is about to explode on the world scene. We trust that this work will inform readers of the present situation of the Temple Mount and will help everyone, no matter what their particular religious faith or understanding of the Bible, appreciate what is presently happening in Israel.

It is our earnest prayer to the God of Abraham, Isaac, and Jacob that, in the midst of the controversies and confusion, our readers will discover the true Messiah of Israel.

Baruch Ha Shem!

Don Stewart and Chuck Missler

Jerusalem, April 1991

Acknowledgements

The authors wish to single out the following people for special thanks:

Kim Stewart: For her wonderful cover concept and design.

A.C. Martin and Associates: For their help with architectural information concerning the design of various temples.

Tuvia Sagiv: For his explanation of why the Temple could have stood on the southern part of the Mount.

Dr. Asher Kaufman: For the many wonderful hours spent in discussion of the actual location of the Temple. We also thank him for the kind permission to use his map of the Temple Mount as well as his unpublished article on the "Foundation Stone."

Temple Institute: For allowing us permission to take photographs of the implements they hope to use in a Third Temple.

Lambert Dolphin and the SRI team: For proving that high tech equipment *can* work to help uncover the past.

Rockefeller Museum: For help in finding rare books and manuscripts dealing with the Temple Mount.

The Coming Temple:

Center Stage For The Final Countdown

CHAPTER ONE

THE TEMPLE MOUNT:
A CENTER OF CONTROVERSY IN
OUR MODERN WORLD

The Land of Israel is at the center of the world; Jerusalem is at the center of the land of Israel; the Temple is at the center of Jerusalem . . .

Midrash Tanhuma, Kedoshim 10

One of the most exciting stories that is occurring in the world today is taking place in the tiny nation of Israel. The story centers around a rocky knoll in the city of Jerusalem known as the Temple Mount. This Mount, which has witnessed some of history's most important events, has become a hotbed of controversy. An ever-increasing struggle is going on for the control of this sacred piece of real estate. The outcome of the struggle will have a monumental impact on the direction of human history for, according to the Bible, events on the Temple Mount will be center stage in the final countdown before the return to earth of Jesus Christ.

Importance of the Temple Mount

The importance of the Temple Mount cannot be overestimated. Three of the world's great religions, Judaism, Islam and Christianity hold the Mount in the highest regard. To Judaism and Islam, the Temple Mount is the holiest site in an area of many "holy sites." In addition, all three religions believe the "Deliverer" will someday come from the East through the Golden Gate onto the Temple Mount. Though the three religions agree that this spot is to witness future great events, they differ on what those events will be.

Islam

The mountain on which the Temple once stood is held sacred by Islam. The Dome of the Rock shrine is built over the "Sacred Rock." Islamic tradition teaches that Allah went up to heaven from this spot after he created all things.

Moslems[1] maintain that this rock fell from heaven about the time that the spirit of prophecy was imparted. They also believe that this rock was also the first place from which the waters of the Flood receded. Moslem tradition has Allah saying, "This is my place and the place of my seat on the day of resurrection."

It is taught that this holy stone wished to accompany the prophet Mohammed to heaven in his "nocturnal flight," but was restrained by the angel Gabriel. The angel Gabriel held the rock so firmly that the impression of his hand is still pointed out to this day.

On the south side of this rock the "footprint" of Mohammed is found. On his famous "Night Flight" where he supposedly ascended into the presence of Allah in the seventh heaven, he left his foot impression in the rock.

Moslems believe the Dome of the Rock contains God's scales for the weighing of the souls of men:

> The Mighty stretched out his hands toward the places that he wished to point out, saying: 'This to the west is the garden of Eden; This to the East is the fire of hell and this is the place of my scales of Justice.'

It is believed the sacred rock also contains the shield of the prophet Mohammed and the saddle of el-Burak-Lightning—the steed on which Mohammed made his night flight from Mecca to Jerusalem. There is also the original copy of Islam's Holy Book, the Koran, the parchment leaves of which are four feet long.

Because of Moslem belief that all these events took place from this rock, the spot is housed by a shrine and held to be sacred. The sanctity and awe with which Moslems regard this spot is beyond description.

The Al-Aqsa Mosque (sometime spelled El Aqsa or Al Aksa) is located some 100 yards south of the Dome of the Rock. This Mosque is the third holiest site in all Islam, behind only Mecca and Medina. Hence, the entire Temple Mount area is considered holy by the Moslems.

Judaism

The Temple Mount, called *Har Ha Bayit* by the Jews, (the Mountain of the House)[2] is also of vital importance to Judaism. Judaism teaches that Abraham, the father of the Hebrew race, took his son Isaac to sacrifice him on the Mount. Later in their history, King David purchased a threshing floor on the Temple Mount that became the site of the First Temple. The Temple became the center point of Jewish religious life with the glory of God residing in the Holy of Holies. The First Temple was destroyed in 586 B.C. but was rebuilt again. The Second Temple was built on that same site but it too was eventually destroyed.

For almost two thousand years the authority of the Temple Mount has been out of Jewish hands. It was not until 1967 that the Jews recaptured the Temple Mount area. However, they returned the control of the Mount back to the Moslems.

Today there are a growing number of voices in Israel who would like to see a Third Temple built upon the Mount. Some believe the building of a Third Temple will usher in the coming of the Messiah. Proposals to rebuild the Temple are a cause for bitter conflict in Jerusalem. Consequently the Temple Mount, the holiest site in all of Judaism, is in the center of a storm of controversy.

Christianity

Finally, the Temple Mount has its importance to the Christian faith. It was at the Temple where the baby Jesus was dedicated. The Temple was where the twelve year old Jesus confounded the elders. The first act of Jesus' public ministry in Jerusalem was the disrupting of the Temple. He turned over the tables of the moneychangers and drove them out. The New Testament records that Jesus taught regularly in the Temple during His public ministry. Jesus also disrupted the Temple a second time shortly before His death on the cross.

When Jesus died on the cross, the New Testament records that the veil of the Temple, separating the holy place from the Holy of Holies, was torn from top to bottom. This signified that man now had direct access to God without the need of any mortal priest as mediator. Jesus has assumed the role of the Great High Priest and has become the mediator between God and man. Hence, Jesus' work of mankind's salvation had an objective witness in the Temple.

The New Testament church began in the Temple courtyard when the Holy Spirit fell upon the believers. The Temple Mount area was very important in the life of Jesus and early Christianity.

Future Interest

Yet the Temple Mount holds an even greater interest to Christians. The Bible predicts that a Third Temple will someday be built.[3] This will trigger a series of events that will climax in the Second Coming of Jesus Christ to earth.

Events, therefore, concerning the possible rebuilding of a Third Temple have monumental interest to Christians.

A Recent Upsurge of Interest

Though always a place of contention, the Temple Mount has received renewed interest in recent years. The Jerusalem *Post* reported that:

> The storm clouds have been gathering for years now, over the Temple Mount. Since 1967, the pressure on successive governments has been unrelenting—yet until recently, quite marginal—to create a Jewish presence on the Mount. But since 1981 . . . some of the most articulate of the Tehiya leadership, have been taking aim at the Temple Mount.
>
> So far, the government, in whose hands the decision rests, has resisted demands and ignored demonstrations seeking Jewish access to the Mount.
>
> But the political wind is stirring across the hilltops of the West Bank—a Jewish presence on the Temple Mount is an affirmation of Jewish sovereignty over all of Jerusalem, over all of the Land of Israel. For those religious Jews. . . ascension to the Temple Mount for prayer is a way of hastening the arrival of the Messiah, who must arrive before the rebuilding of the Temple can commence. . .
>
> But for Jerusalemites, who live in this melting pot of unmeltable faiths, the simmering issues are beginning to boil.[4]

Louis Rapoport, the Jewish writer, stated the matter correctly, "Politically there is no place in the Middle East as potentially explosive as the Temple Mount."[5]

Temple Mount in the Headlines

The Temple Mount has repeatedly found itself in the headlines in recent years. Some of them include:

. **Armed Terrorists Attempt to Scale Mount**

Israel Investigates Jewish Extremists in Mosque Plot

A Time Bomb at the City's Heart

Bloody Monday on the Temple Mount

Time for a New Temple?

On October 22, 1990, *Newsweek* magazine made the following comment:

> In Jerusalem, writes the city's former deputy mayor, Meron Benvenisti, "Violence courts violence in a perpetual magic circle . . . And at its heart, a time bomb with a destructive force of apocalyptic dimensions is ticking, in the form of the Temple Mount." The hill at the eastern edge of Jerusalem's Old City, sacred to both Jews and Muslims is the focus of irreconcilable and communal strife.
>
> The Temple Mount commands no ancient trade routes. It straddles no vital water supplies. Yet it sits on a rich vein of memory and meaning. . . . In Palestinian refugee camps throughout the Middle East, schoolchildren learn to paint images of the dome on the walls of their playgrounds . . .6
>
> In recent years this arrangement [the status quo] has been challenged by rising Jewish ultranationalism and the intifada. The Temple Mount Faithful, the fringe group whose plans to march on the mount last week angered Palestinians, believe the Messiah's arrival can be

hastened by building a temple now. They have already carved a three-ton cornerstone—without the use of metal chisels, as the Bible instructs. "The Temple Mount is our religious and spiritual center," says Faithful leader Gershon Solomon. "We are sorry, but the mosque must be moved." The Faithful are reviled by many Israelis. . . . Gradually the police have granted the group more latitude. A few months ago small groups of Faithful were allowed on the Temple Mount—though the courts, as they did last week, still forbid them from laying a cornerstone there. Israel has snuffed out violent plots by other Jewish extremists including one 1985 scheme to blow up the Muslim shrines.[7]

The Temple Mount will remain in the headlines because the Bible says it holds a strategic position in coming world events.

Center Stage: Past, Present and Future

As we look at the story of the Temple Mount we will discover how it has been the center stage for many events in our past. In addition, it remains the center of controversy in our present world. As we delve into the subject of Bible prophecy we will find the Temple Mount will be center stage for the final countdown for humanity. The Temple Mount, therefore, is a subject that should interest all of us for the future of this planet will revolve around events that happen on this sacred piece of real estate.

Endnotes

1. Throughout the book we will use the spelling Moslem rather than Muslim. Both are considered acceptable.

2. The Hebrew הר הבית has come to refer to the entire Temple Mount. Dr. Asher Kaufman has investigated the original meaning of the term during the Second Temple period. He concludes that *Har Habbayit* was the name given to the outer sanctified court of the Temple, not the Temple area itself. "The Meaning of Har Habbayit and its Northern Gate." Niv Hamidrashia 18/19 1984/1985.

3. For a defense of this position see Appendix 1.

4. Robert Rosenberg, Special Report: Target Temple Mount, Jerusalem *Post,* Local Supplement, Friday, September 30, 1983.

5. *Jewish Digest,* Sept. 1982, p. 28.

6. See our pictures in the photo section.

7. *Newsweek,* October 22, 1990.

CHAPTER TWO

THE RISE AND FALL OF THE FIRST TEMPLE

> There is an outcropping of starkly bare rough limestone rock in Jerusalem which for thirty centuries past has gripped the minds and hearts of sons of men as being the most sacred spot on earth. Known to the Jews as the Temple Mount and to the Moslems as the Noble Sanctuary. Tradition and legend blend together where it is difficult to separate the two. . . . Few places in the world have been . . . as sacred as this city, this flattened mountain and this rock. While the world lasts and as long as the sons of men believe that one spot on it is more sacred and hallowed than another, this will remain so.[1]

The story of the Temple Mount goes back at least four thousand years to God's dealings with a man named Abraham.

Today there are three great world religions that believe in only one God (Judaism, Christianity and Islam). Each religion has an outstanding figure whom they revere. To the Jews it is Moses, the giver of the Law. To the Moslems it is Mohammed, the last and greatest of the prophets. To the Christians it is Jesus, God's only Son and the promised Messiah.

Yet each of these three religions trace their beginnings back four thousand years ago to one man, Abraham.

Jesus, Moses and Mohammed were all physical descendants of Abraham. Forty centuries ago, God called this man out of a sinful culture and made him promises that still apply today:

> Now the Lord said to Abram: "Get out of your country, from your kindred and from your father's house, to a land I will show you. I will make you a great nation; I will bless you and make your name great; and you shall be a blessing. I will bless those who bless you, and I will curse him who curses you; and in you all the families of the earth shall be blessed" (Genesis 12:1-3).

God showed Abraham the borders of the land that was to belong to him and his descendants:

> And the Lord said to Abram, after Lot had separated from him: "Lift your eyes now and look to the place where you are—northward, southward, eastward, and westward; for all the land which you see I give to you and your descendants forever. And I will make your descendants as the dust of the earth; so that if a man could number the dust of the earth, then your descendants also could be numbered. Arise and walk the land through its length and width, for I give it to you" (Genesis 13:14-17).

The promises made to Abraham and his descendants are everlasting:

> 'And I will establish My covenant between Me and you and your descendants after you in their generations, for an everlasting covenant, to be God to you and your descendants after you. And I will give to you and your descendants after you the land in which you are a stranger, all the land of Canaan, as an everlasting possession; and I will be their God' (Genesis 17:7,8).

This covenant, or agreement, that God made with Abraham's descendants cannot be revoked.

God's Promises

In these passages God made the following promises to Abraham and his descendants:

1. A great nation will spring from Abraham
2. Abraham's name shall be blessed
3. He shall be a blessing to all nations
4. Those who bless Abraham's people will be blessed
5. Those who curse Abraham's people will be cursed
6. His descendants will be countless
7. His descendants will inherit this promised land
8. The land belongs to them forever

Against all odds, all of these promises have been literally fulfilled. The fact that they have all been fulfilled as promised demonstrates the existence and faithfulness of God.[2]

Promise of a Son

Among the promises God made to Abraham was that of a son. The Bible says that the Lord appeared to Abraham when he and his wife Sarah were advanced in age and promised they would have a son the next year. Sarah laughed when she overheard the promise:

> And Sarah was listening in the tent door behind them. Now Abraham and Sarah were old, well advanced in age; and Sarah had passed the age of childbearing. Therefore Sarah laughed within herself, saying, "After I have grown old, shall I have pleasure, my lord being old also?" And the Lord said to Abraham, "Why did Sarah laugh, saying, 'Shall I surely bear a child, since I am old?' Is anything too hard for the Lord?" (Genesis 18:1,10-14).

As God had promised Abraham and Sarah had a son. They named him Isaac, which means "laughter."

Later, when Isaac had grown into a man, God asked Abraham to make the supreme sacrifice. After waiting so long for a son to be born, the Bible records that God told Abraham to take this beloved son of promise and offer him as a burnt offering:

> Now it came to pass after these things that God tested Abraham, and said to him, "Abraham!" And he said, "Here I am." And he said, "Take now your son, your only son Isaac, whom you love, and go to the land of Moriah, and offer him there as a burnt offering on one of the mountains of which I shall tell you" (Genesis 22:1,2).

Mt. Moriah

Abraham acted in obedience to God and went on a three day journey to the site which God had chosen. The site that God brought Abraham would later become the city of Jerusalem. The exact location on Mt. Moriah is believed by some to be the Temple Mount.[3]

When they reached the mountain that God had chosen, Abraham was prepared to sacrifice Isaac:

> But Isaac spoke to Abraham his father and said . . . "Look, the fire and the wood, but where is the lamb for a burnt offering?" And Abraham said, "My son, God will provide for Himself the lamb for the burnt offering" (Genesis 22:7,8).

At the last moment, God stayed the hand of Abraham as he was about to sacrifice his son. Instead, Abraham offered a ram as a sacrifice on Mt. Moriah. There Abraham appropriately named the spot:

> And Abraham called the name of the place, The-Lord-Will-Provide; as it is said to this day, "In the Mount of the Lord it shall be provided" (Genesis 22:14).

Abraham looked forward to the day when God would provide another sacrifice on that exact spot.[4]

Promise Fulfilled

As God had promised, a great nation sprung from Abraham through his son Isaac. After this nation spent four hundred years as slaves in Egypt God delivered them with His mighty power in the Exodus. He then set them on the way to the Promised Land.

Under Moses' leadership in the wilderness, God established a place where they could go to commune with Him. This was the Tabernacle or tent of meeting.[5]

The Tabernacle

The Lord gave Moses the commandment to build the place of meeting: "Let them make Me a sanctuary; that I may dwell among them" (Exodus 25:8).

It is important to note that Moses did not suggest to God that a Tabernacle should be built and then God agreed to occupy it. It is just the opposite. God lovingly looked down upon His people as He directed them toward the Promised Land. He would not only guide them, He would dwell with them.

Consequently, He instructed Moses to build the Tabernacle in the midst of the camp, just as a Bedouin chieftain would pitch his tent in the midst of an encampment.

The Tabernacle was the place where God met His people. It was basically a huge tent about 45 feet long divided into two parts by a veil of richly decorated linen. The Tabernacle was made from the skins of rams and goats. The first room, upon entering was the Holy Place. It was about 30 feet by 15 feet in size. In the center of the room, before the veil was the altar of incense standing about three feet high. On it was placed charcoal and a

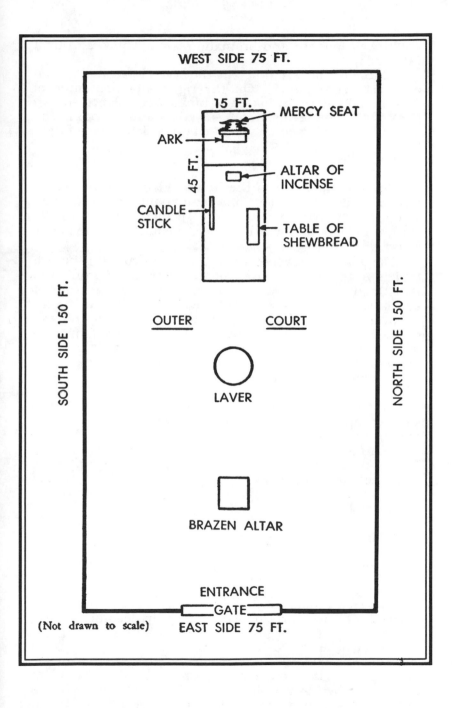

mixture of incense and aromatic resins. This was burnt twice a day.

On the left of this altar was the seven branched golden candlestick (Menorah). On the right was the Table of Showbread where 12 loaves of bread were placed in two piles of six. The bread, which served as a memorial to the twelve tribes of Israel, was renewed every Sabbath day.

Holy of Holies

Beyond the veil was the holiest place known as the Holy of Holies. Its dimensions were about 15 cubits each way (a cubit was approximately 18 inches long). In the Holy of Holies was the Ark of the Covenant and the Mercy Seat.

The Ark was a wooden chest made to contain the two tablets of the Law (the ten commandments), Aaron's rod that budded and a pot of manna. The Ark, made out of acacia wood, was also called the Ark of the Law. It was about four feet long and two and one half feet high. It was covered inside and outside with gold. There were four rings fixed to its side through which two carrying poles were passed. It was placed under the care of the Levites, who were exempt from military duties.

On the top of the Ark was the Mercy Seat that had two golden Cherubim with outstretched wings at each end. The Cherubim, of which little is known, were winged celestial creatures whose purpose was to guard and protect.

The Mercy Seat received its name because the High Priest, once a year on the Day of Atonement, sprinkled it with the blood of the sacrifice. This was the most sacred place in the entire Sanctuary. It was the visible throne of the invisible presence of God.

God Communicated to Man

From the Holy of Holies God spoke to His people:

And there I will meet with you, and I will speak with you from above the mercy seat, from between the two cherubim which are on the ark of the Testimony, of all things which I will give you in commandment to the children of Israel (Exodus 25:22).

The Tabernacle was moved each day as the children of Israel marched in the wilderness. Every day they moved, the Tabernacle was dismantled and carried on poles. At night the tribes were encamped in a square formation with the Tabernacle erected at the center.

The Tabernacle was only a temporary structure, looking forward to the day when a permanent house of the Lord could be built.

Promised Land

Through the leadership of Joshua, Moses' successor, the children of Israel entered the land of Canaan (the Promised land). After the conquest of Canaan, the Tabernacle remained in Shiloh, some 20 miles north of Jerusalem, through the time of the Judges.[6]

The Desire of David

One of the greatest figures in the history of Israel was King David. David captured the city of Jerusalem from the Jebusites and was crowned king of Israel in the city of Hebron. He solidified the nation by making Jerusalem its capital. David brought the Ark of the Covenant to Jerusalem and placed it in the Tabernacle.

King David observed that while he lived in a house of cedar, God's presence still was in curtains (the Tabernacle). Hence, David conceived a plan for a more permanent structure to be built, a Temple.

God told king David that a Temple was to be built, but not by him. David was not to be the one who would build the Temple because he was a man of war. That job would belong to his son, Solomon.

The original command for building the Temple was given by God, "He shall build a house for my name" (2 Samuel 7:13).

Memorial

The fact that other nations had temples and Israel did not is not the reason it was built. The Temple was to be a memorial to Israel to turn her heart away from the idols of her contemporaries. The Temple would provide for the people an incentive not to practice the same evil things as the Canaanites.

Araunah's Threshing Floor

The place for the site of the Temple was chosen before the reign of Solomon:

> So the Lord sent a plague upon Israel from the
> morning till the appointed time . . . And the angel
> stretched out his hand over Jerusalem to destroy it, the
> Lord relented from the destruction, and said to the angel
> who was destroying the people, "It is enough; now
> restrain Your hand." And the angel of the Lord was by the
> threshing floor of Araunah the Jebusite . . . And Gad came
> that day to David and said to him, "Go up, erect an altar
> to the Lord on the threshing floor of Araunah the
> Jebusite." . . . And David built there an altar unto the Lord,
> and offered burnt offerings and peace offerings. So the
> Lord heeded the prayers for the land, and the plague was
> withdrawn from Israel (2 Samuel 24:15,16,18,25).

King David purchased the threshing floor of Araunah
(alternative spelling Ornan) as the site of the First
Temple.[7] There he built an altar and offered a sacrifice. The
place was on Mt. Moriah, the same site, many believe,
where one thousand years earlier God stopped Abraham
from sacrificing Isaac.

The Construction of the Temple

After the death of his father David, Solomon ordered
the building of the First Temple:

> You know that my father David could not build a house
> for the name of the Lord his God because of the wars
> which were fought against him on every side until the
> Lord put his foes under the soles of his feet (1 Kings 5:3).

The building of the First Temple was a monumental
task. Phoenician craftsmen were employed to build the
Temple.[8] Construction began in the fourth year of
Solomon's reign and took seven years:[9]

> Then King Solomon raised up a labor force out of all
> Israel; and the labor force was thirty thousand men . . .
> Solomon selected seventy thousand men to bear burdens,
> eighty thousand to quarry stone in the mountains, and
> three thousand six hundred to oversee them (1 Kings
> 5:13;2 Chronicles 2:2).

The stones were hewn from a quarry and brought to
the Temple site:

> And the temple, when it was being built, was built with
> stone finished at the quarry, so that no hammer or chisel

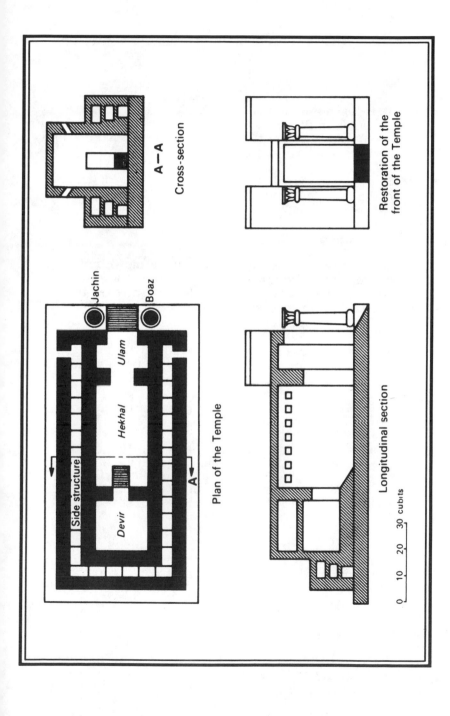

A – A
Cross-section

Restoration of the
front of the Temple

Jachin

Boaz

Ulam

Hekhal

Side structure

Devir

A

Plan of the Temple

Longitudinal section

0 10 20 30 cubits

or any iron tool was heard in the temple while it was being
built (1 Kings 6:7).

Dedication

After the completion of the Temple, it was dedicated by
King Solomon in 953 B.C. In his prayer Solomon realized
that the Temple was not the dwelling place of God but only
representative of His Person:

> But will God indeed dwell on the earth? Behold, heaven
> and the heaven of heavens cannot contain You. How
> much less this Temple which I have built (1 Kings 8:27).

No Idols

The feature that set apart the Solomonic Temple from
other Temples in the ancient world is that there were no
idols in it. It contained only the Mercy Seat over the Ark
and the Cherubim overshadowing the Mercy Seat. This
declared to the world that idols are unnecessary for God to
be present.

The God of Israel was not localized in any sense.
Neither was He bound to any other form such as the Ark.
The Temple, therefore, was not necessary because of God's
nature. He did not need it.

One thousand years later, the martyr Stephen said to
an unruly crowd:

> But Solomon built Him a house. However the Most High
> does not dwell in temples made with hands, as the
> prophet says: Heaven is My throne, and the earth is my
> footstool. What house will you build for Me? says the
> Lord or what is the place of My rest? Has not My hand
> made all these things? (Acts 7:47-50).

The Temple was built to meet the limitations and needs
of God's people. It emphasized the way of salvation to
those who asked His forgiveness and represented to the
believers assurance of the grace of God for their joy and
blessing (1 Kings 8:27-30).

Symbolic Meanings

The Old Testament says that the Temple has many
symbolic meanings.[10] The Temple symbolized the hearing
ear of God (1 Kings 8:28,29). It was also a place of refuge for

the stranger (1 Kings 8:41-43). The Temple is the house of prayer for all people where all nations of the earth should fear God (Isaiah 56:7).

After the Temple was built the Tabernacle was dismantled. Its fate is unknown. It may have been stored in a room under the Temple Mount.

Solomon's Apostasy

Late in his life, King Solomon fell spiritually away from the Lord. He married many foreign wives who brought in their idols to Jerusalem and to the Temple. This set the stage for the dividing of the kingdom.

When Solomon died his son Rehoboam became king of Israel. The nation, however, was on a spiritual decline. Rehoboam's policies caused the kingdom to be divided into north (Israel) and south (Judah).

Jereboam, the first king of Israel, built two substitute places of worship, one in Bethel and one in Dan for fear the people would return to Jerusalem. The northern kingdom remained in idolatry until its captivity in 721 B.C.

Invasion of Shishak

The southern kingdom of Judah also fell into sin. Consequently, God allowed Pharaoh Shishak of Egypt to come down and plunder the Temple.

> And it happened in the fifth year of King Rehoboam, that Shishak, king of Egypt came against Jerusalem because they transgressed against the Lord. . . So Shishak king of Egypt came up against Jerusalem and took away the treasures of the house of the Lord and the treasures of the kings house; he took everything. He also carried away the gold shields which Solomon had made (2 Chronicles 12:2,9).

The history of the First Temple in Jerusalem is covered in the books of the Kings and Chronicles. We will consider only some of the important events surrounding it.

Ahaz

One of the worst kings of Judah was Ahaz. He desecrated the Temple and robbed it of its treasures. Ahaz sent the Temple treasures along with his own to the Assyrian monarch Tiglath-Pileser III to secure his aid in an alliance against Israel and Syria. Ahaz then went to Damascus and had a copy of their altar made and brought to Jerusalem. There he placed it before the altar of the Lord and made a sacrifice on this pagan replica. He also closed the Temple and broke up the vessels.

Restoration Under Hezekiah

The Temple was later restored under the leadership of a good King named Hezekiah:

> Go up to Hilkiah the high priest, that he may count the money which has been brought into the house of the Lord, which the doorkeepers have gathered from the people. And let them deliver it into the hand of those doing the work, who are the overseers in the house of the Lord; let them give it to those who are in the house of the Lord doing the work, to repair the damages of the house— (2 Kings 22:4,5).

Hezekiah opened the doors and restored the vessels which Ahaz had put away. Unfortunately, Hezekiah was lifted up with pride and made alliances with foreign nations. This assured the eventual downfall of Jerusalem (2 Chronicles 32:24).

Idolatry Increases

Hezekiah's son Manasseh built idolatrous altars in the Temple courts and placed a pagan image in the Temple. God punished Manasseh by sending him to Babylon. When Manasseh repented he was returned to Jerusalem where he repaired the altar.

Manasseh's son Amon followed in the idolatrous example of his father. He worshiped an image of his father. After two years his servants assassinated him. The people then killed the assassins and made Josiah king.

A reformation took place under King Josiah. Josiah ordered the Temple repaired. The stone work was repaired and certain timbers replaced. Josiah removed the idols from the Temple and restored two of the temple's courts. He also had the Ark of the Covenant put back into the Holy of Holies (2 Chronicles 35:3).[11] The people, however, did not truly turn to the Lord in repentance.

Jehoiakim

The reign of Jehoiakim was the beginning of the end for Judah. Nebuchadnezzar king of Babylon made Jehoiakim his subject. After three years Jehoiakim rebelled and Nebuchadnezzar laid siege to the city (2 Kings 24:1).

His son Jehoiachin also did evil. The Temple vessels were taken to Babylon while Jehoiachin and his family were taken prisoner along with ten thousand captives including the skilled craftsmen. Only the poorest of the poor remained in the land.

Destruction of First Temple

The prophet Jeremiah predicted the destruction of Jerusalem and a seventy year captivity of the people. He also pronounced judgment on those who destroyed her, Babylon:

> "And the whole land shall be a desolation and an astonishment, and these nations shall serve the king of Babylon seventy years. Then it will come to pass, when seventy years are completed, that I will punish the king of Babylon and that nation, the land of the Chaldeans, for their iniquity," says the Lord; 'and I will make it a perpetual desolation (Jeremiah 25:11,12).

Despite the reforms and revivals the destruction of the First Temple was carried out as predicted:

> Now in the fifth month on the seventh day of the month (which was the nineteenth year of King Nebuchadnezzar king of Babylon), Nebuzaradan the captain of the guard, a servant of the king of Babylon come to Jerusalem. He burned the house of the Lord and the king's house; all the houses of Jerusalem, that is all the house of the great men he burned with fire (2 Kings 25:8,9).

Nebuchadnezzar king of Babylon destroyed the city and Temple in 586 B.C. as Jeremiah predicted. Babylon was also judged. In 539 B.C. Babylon fell to the Medes and the Persians (Daniel 5).

Summary

The existence of the First Temple was relatively short-lived (less than 400 years) because the people turned their back on God. Though they were judged for their sin, and expelled from their land, God, who is rich in mercy, promised them they would return.

Endnotes

1. Solomon Steckoll, *The Temple Mount*, London. Tom Stacey Lt., 1972, p. 9.

2. Don Stewart, *The Ten Wonders of the Bible*, Orange California, Dart Press, 1990.

3. Not all scholars agree. There is good reason to believe that Abraham took Isaac to Golgotha (Calvary) which is on the higher ground. Furthermore, during the time of Abraham, there was an existing Jebusite city on the southern slope of the Temple Mount. It is unlikely that Abraham would have taken Isaac to sacrifice him directly above that city. See our discussion and diagram in Chapter Ten.

4. Two thousand years after Abraham offered Isaac, another Father sacrificed His Son on that same ground (John 3:16).

5. The Tabernacle is also referred to as a Temple (1 Samuel 1:9).

6. Shiloh was destroyed by the Philistines (1050 B.C.). It will probably be the site for the last Temple. See our discussion in Appendix 5.

7. When the Tabernacle was originally set up in Jerusalem, it was placed somewhere other than the Temple Mount. There would have been no need for King David to first buy the threshing floor from Araunah if they were already on that site.

8. Freemasonry claims its origin began here with the construction of the First Temple.

9. See our discussion on the wealth of the Temple in Appendix 3.

10. Many symbolic meanings of the Temple have been suggested ranging from the sublime to the bizarre. Attempts have been made to correlate the Temple dimensions to the Great Pyramid in Egypt. For a Christian perspective of the architecture see Nancy Missler "Way of Agape." Koinonia House, Box 881, Big Bear Lake, California 92315.

11. This is the last biblical reference to the Ark of the Covenant. Its whereabouts, to this day, remain a mystery.

CHAPTER THREE

RETURN, REBUILDING AND A SECOND DESTRUCTION

> How lonely sits the city that was full of people! How like a widow is she, who was great among the nations! The princess among the provinces has become a slave. . . Judah has gone into captivity, under affliction and hard servitude; she dwells among the nations, she finds no rest; all her persecutors overtake her in dire straits.
>
> Lamentations of Jeremiah 1:1,3

After the First Temple was destroyed and the nation was carried off into Babylon, some people still came to Jerusalem to offer sacrifices:

> Certain men came from Shechem, from Shiloh, and from Samaria, eighty men with beards shaved and their clothes torn, having cut themselves, with offerings and incense in their hand, to bring them to the house of the Lord (Jeremiah 41:5).

Yet there was no Temple in which they could offer their sacrifices.

The Return Predicted

The prophet Daniel, while in captivity in Babylon, read the prophecies of Jeremiah concerning the predicted return from captivity:

> In the first year of Darius, the son of Ahasuerus, of the lineage of the Medes, who was made king over the realm of the Chaldeans—in the first year of his reign I, Daniel, understood by the books the number of the years specified by the word of the Lord, given through Jeremiah the prophet, that He would accomplish seventy years in the desolations of Jerusalem (Daniel 9:1,2).

Realizing the captivity was about to be completed, Daniel began to pray. God then gave him a further revelation of what was to happen in the future in the prophecy of the seventy weeks (Daniel 9:24-27).[1]

The Return

After seventy years of Jerusalem being desolated the people returned to the land. The prophecy of Jeremiah was literally fulfilled. For seventy years the people were removed from the land for forgetting to give it rest:

> And this whole land shall be a desolation and an astonishment, and these nations shall serve the king of Babylon seventy years. Then it will come to pass, when seventy years are completed, that I will punish the king of Babylon, and that nation, the land of the Chaldeans, for their iniquity,' says the Lord: 'and I will make it a perpetual desolation' (Jeremiah 25:11,12).

The Scriptures commanded that every seventh year the land should be allowed to rest. The people, however, ignored this command. For 490 years they worked the land. This meant that during this period there should have been seventy years in which the land was made to rest.[2] Because the people did not observe those seventy years, God took them away from the land for that exact period of time to fulfill His commandment:

> Then they burned the house of God, broke down the wall of Jerusalem, burned all its palaces with fire, and destroyed all it precious possessions. And those who escaped from the sword he carried to Babylon, where they became servants to him and his sons until the reign of the kingdom of Persia, to fulfill the word of the Lord by the mouth of Jeremiah, until the land had enjoyed her Sabbaths. As long as she lay desolate she kept Sabbath, to fulfill seventy years (2 Chronicles 36:21).

Prophecy Concerning Cyrus

One of the most amazing prophecies in the entire Bible concerns the return of the Jews from captivity and the building of the Second Temple. Isaiah the prophet, writing in 700 B.C., records the Lord as saying:

> Who says to Jerusalem, 'You shall be inhabited.' . . .
> Who says of Cyrus, 'He is My shepherd, and he shall

perform all My pleasure, even saying to Jerusalem, "You shall be built," and to the temple, "Your foundation shall be laid." '

Thus says the Lord to His anointed, to Cyrus . . . 'I will give you treasures of darkness and hidden riches of secret places, that you may know that I am the Lord, Who call you by your name, am the God of Israel. For Jacob's My servant's sake, and Israel My elect, I have even called you by your name; I have named you though you have not known Me' (Isaiah 44:26-45:4).

From this passage we can see the following specific predictions:

1. Judah would return from captivity.
2. The rebuilding of the city of Jerusalem would begin.
3. The foundation of the Temple would be laid.
4. It would be accomplished by Cyrus who is addressed by name.
5. Cyrus will do this even though he is not a believer.

According to this prophecy, Cyrus was the person the Lord stirred up. He was the one who would perform the task of the Lord even though he did not personally know Him. Cyrus was merely an instrument in God's plan.

When the prophecy of Isaiah was given the Temple was still standing, the city of Jerusalem had not yet been destroyed, and the people were not in exile. Furthermore, Cyrus hadn't even been born! Yet all these predictions were literally fulfilled as Isaiah prophesied.[3]

Response of Cyrus

There is non-biblical evidence that Cyrus was aware of the prophecies. The first-century Jewish writer Flavius Josephus writes:

by reading the book which Isaiah left behind of his prophecies; for this prophet said that God had spoken thus to him in a secret vision—'My will is, that Cyrus, whom I have appointed to be king over many and great nations, send back my people to their own land, and build my temple.' Accordingly, when Cyrus read this, and admired the divine power, an earnest desire and ambition seized upon him to fulfil what was so written.[4]

After the Jews returned to Jerusalem a campaign was begun to rebuild the Temple:

"Thus speaks the Lord of hosts saying: 'This people says, 'The time has not come, the time that the Lord's house should be built." ' Then the word of the Lord came by Haggai saying, "Is it time for you yourselves to dwell in paneled houses and this temple to lie in ruins? . . . Go to the mountains and bring wood and build the temple, that I may take pleasure in it and be glorified" (Haggai 1:2-4,8).

Haggai predicted the Second Temple would be more glorious than the First:[5]

"The glory of this latter temple shall be greater than the former," says the Lord of hosts. 'And in this place I will give peace,' says the Lord of hosts (Haggai 2:9).

Two years after the release from captivity the foundation was laid by a man named Sheshbazzar (Ezra 5:16).

Nehemiah

Nehemiah held the office of cupbearer to King Artaxerxes I in the Persian capital of Susa. A relative from Jerusalem visited him and gave a report of the sad condition of Jerusalem. He told him how vulnerable the city was to attack because the walls were still in rubble. This so disturbed Nehemiah that he decided to visit Jerusalem. The King gave him permission to leave and provided him with an armed escort. Nehemiah also had royal letters ordering the provincial authorities to provide him with timber and other materials he required.

He arrived in Jerusalem in 445 B.C. and by moonlight began to inspect the walls and gates. Nehemiah then called the leading citizens and produced the letters from the king. The people accepted him as their governor. Nehemiah then outlined his plans for the urgent task of rebuilding the fortifications and securing the city. Work was done on a voluntary basis.

Nehemiah's arrival provided a new enthusiasm to the those in Jerusalem but it also caused some hostile reaction. The main adversaries were Sanballat, the local governor of Samaria, Geshem, the leader of the Edomites, and a wealthy Jew named Tobiah.

They began by verbally attacking the project but when the walls were half way complete they resorted to force. Nehemiah countered with full-time armed patrols.   Each worker was given a weapon to defend himself (Nehemiah 4:18).

As the prophecy stated the rebuilding of the Temple was started in Cyrus' reign:

> Now in the second month of the second year of their coming to the house of God at Jerusalem, Zerubbabel the son of Shealtiel, Jeshua, the son of Jozadak, and the rest of their brethren the priests and Levites, and all those who had come out of captivity to Jerusalem began work and appointed the Levites from twenty years old and above to oversee the work of the house of the Lord . . . When the builders laid the foundation of the temple of the Lord, the priests stood in their apparel with trumpets, and the Levites, the sons of Asaph, with cymbals, to praise the Lord, according to the ordinance of David king of Israel. And they sang responsively, praising and giving thanks to the Lord: "For He is good, for His mercy endures forever toward Israel." Then all the people shouted with a great shout, when they praised the Lord, because the foundation of the house of the Lord was laid (Ezra 3:8-11).

Second Temple Built

The successors of Cyrus, Darius (522-486 B.C.) and Artaxerxes I (465-423 B.C.) saw through the completion of the rebuilding of the city and the Temple. A Second Temple was eventually completed in 517 B.C. under the leadership of Zerubbabel and inspired by the prophet Haggai. The Book of Ezra records:

> And this house was finished . . . and the children of Israel . . . kept the dedication of this house with joy (Ezra 6:15,16).

Though there was rejoicing at the new Temple those who had seen the glory of the previous one were moved to tears:

> But many of the priests and Levites and head of the father's houses, who were old men, who had seen the first temple, wept with a loud voice when the foundation of this temple was laid before their eyes; yet many shouted aloud for joy (Ezra 3:12).

Poor as this structure was by comparison, God was pleased with it and He again took up His abode with His people. However this Temple was without the Ark of the Covenant. A seven branched Menorah stood in the Holy place instead of the ten lampstands in Solomon's Temple.

The apocryphal book of 1 Maccabees provides details of its furnishing:

> They renewed the sacred vessels and the lamp-stand, and brought the altar of incense, and the table to the temple. They burnt incense on the altar and lit the lamps on the lamp-stand to shine within the temple. When they put the Bread of the Presence on the table and hung the curtain their work was completed (1 Maccabees 4:49,50).

Of the Temple built by Zerubbabel little is known. It is difficult to determine, even in general outline, the stages in the historical development of the Temple Mount and its fortifications during the time from Zerubbabel to the start of Herod's building project. The literary sources are not clear, and archaeological data are very few and problematic.

Desecration by Antiochus

The Second Temple was desecrated in 167 B.C. by a Seleucid ruler named Antiochus the IV. Antiochus took upon himself the name Epiphanes ("coming"). He tried to enforce worship of the Greek gods. Antiochus desecrated the Temple by slaughtering a pig on the altar and then placing a pagan image in the Holy of Holies. He also carried away the Temple treasures.

The Book of 1 Maccabees records some of Antiochus' deeds:

> On his return from the conquest of Egypt, in the year 143 (169 B.C.), Antiochus marched with a strong force against Israel and Jerusalem. In his arrogance he entered the temple and carried off the golden altar, the lamp-stand with all its equipment, the table for the Bread of the Presence, the sacred cups and bowls, the golden censers, the curtain and the crowns. He stripped off the gold plating from the Temple front. He seized the silver, gold, and precious vessels, and whatever secret treasures he found, and took them all with him when he left for his own country (1 Maccabees 1:21).

Maccabean Revolt

Jewish leader Judas Maccabees revolted against the Syrians. The revolt succeeded and the Temple was purified.[6]

> Then Judas said to his brothers, "Our enemies have been crushed; let us go up to cleanse the sanctuary and rededicate it." Thus all the army gathered together and went up to Mount Zion. And they saw the Temple desolated, the altar profaned, and the gates burned down. In the courtyard they saw bushes grown as in a thicket. They saw the priests chambers ruined. Then they ripped their clothes, and mourned with a great lamentation and sprinkled themselves with ashes (1 Maccabees 4:36-40).

From 165 B.C to 63 B.C. the Hasmoneans[7] ruled from an independent Jerusalem.

Enter Rome

One hundred years later, Israel fell into Roman rule in 63 B.C. The Roman General Pompey captured the city of Jerusalem. When he arrived at the Temple he found it empty. At the beginning of the second century A.D. the Roman historian Tacitus wrote:

> Pompey was the first Roman who subdued the Jews. By right of conquest he entered their temple. It is a fact well known, that he found no image, no statue, no symbolical representation of the Deity: the whole presented a naked dome; the sanctuary was unadorned and simple. By Pompey's orders the walls of the city were levelled to the ground, but the temple was left entire.

Four Other Temples

During the time of the Second Temple there were four other Temples outside Jerusalem that served the needs of the Jews who were outside of Judea. Two were in Egypt: one in the city of Elephantine and the other in northern Egypt. Another Temple was built by the Samaritans at Mt. Gerizim while the fourth was built west of Amman in Transjordan. Israeli archaeologist Benjamin Mazar writes of these structures:

> The construction of these temples was undertaken in large part to meet the needs of a large Jewish population

already widespread from its homeland, and to fulfill the ambitions of the leaders of these Jewish communities outside of Judea. Although they were inspired by the Second Temple in Jerusalem, built during the Persian period . . . the new structures were significantly different in architectural plan and execution showing the influence of contemporary style.[8]

Herod

In 37 B.C. an Idumean named Herod the Great was appointed king over Israel by Rome. Though Herod was very cruel he was a brilliant builder.

About twenty years before the birth of Jesus Christ an enlargement of the Second Temple was undertaken during the reign of Herod the Great. This enlargement was still going on during the life of Jesus. This enlargement of the Second Temple became known as Herod's Temple.[9] It was at Herod's Temple where Jesus spent His ministry.

The Scripture is silent as to the building of this Temple. It did not have the blessing of God as did the smaller Temple built by Zerubbabel.

History tells us that Herod suggested to the Jews that he should be given the right to replace the Temple built by Zerubbabel. He told them that this new Temple would be more worthy of the name of their God if it were built. Herod, however, was an evil man with no religious faith whatsoever. He cared not for the Jews or their God. What then was his reason for building a Temple? The best answer is that he built it as his memorial, to perpetuate his name. Herod knew the people hated him and that after his death he soon would be forgotten. If this be the reason that the Temple was enlarged then it certainly was not within the plan and purpose of God.

The Ark of the Covenant and the Shekinah glory was missing from Herod's Temple. The ministry of Jesus was only in the outer court, not the inner sanctuary. God was not there; it had become a den of thieves.

Doubled in Size

Herod had to reconstruct the Temple that was already standing. The enlarged Temple was twice the size as the First. Herod enlarged the Temple area by constructing a vast platform around it. The Temple area contained the Antonia Fortress at the northwest corner. This is where

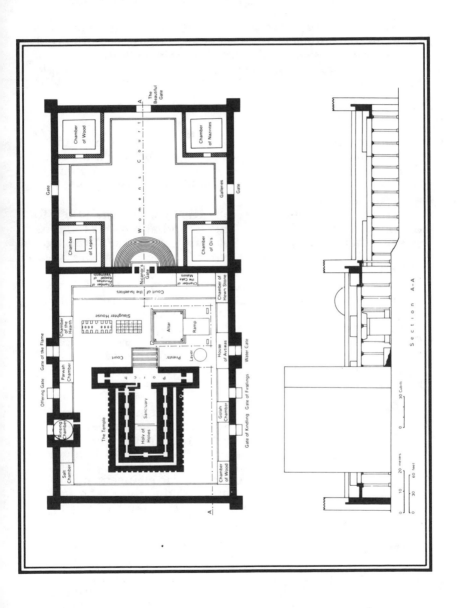

Section A-A

the Procurator lived as well as where the Roman garrison was housed.

First century historian Flavius Josephus remarked that the high priests' robes were kept there as a token of subjection to Rome. Herod's Temple was known for its beauty. The sages said, "He who has not seen the Temple has not seen a beautiful building."

New Testament Period

Important events in the life of Jesus Christ took place in the Temple area. Jesus was brought to the Temple to be dedicated at the age of eight days (Luke 2:27). When He was twelve Luke records that Jesus confounded the elders with His wisdom (Luke 2:41-50).

When Jesus was tempted by the devil he was taken to the pinnacle of the Temple. This is probably what today is the southeast corner, or "Solomon's Stables." This was most likely the same spot where James was martyred (Acts 12).

One of the most famous incidents in the life and ministry of Jesus took place in the Temple area. Many people think of Jesus as someone meek and mild who would never raise His voice or be upset at anything. Consequently, they have a hard time understanding the Gospel accounts of Him going into the temple and disrupting the activities of the moneychangers. John records what occurred:[10]

> Now the Passover of the Jews was at hand, and Jesus went up to Jerusalem. And He found in the temple those who sold oxen and sheep and doves, and the moneychangers doing business. When He had made a whip of cords, He drove all out of the temple, with the sheep and the oxen, and poured out the changers' money and overturned the tables. And He said to those who sold doves, 'Take these things away! Do not make My Father's house a house of merchandise!' (John 2:13-16).

Destruction Predicted

Rejected by those for whom He came, Jesus predicted that the Second Temple would be destroyed. In the last week of His life, Jesus pronounced judgment upon the Temple:

> Then Jesus went out and departed from the temple, and His disciples came to Him to show Him the buildings

of the temple. And Jesus said to them, "Do you not see all these things? Assuredly, I say to you, not one stone shall be left here upon another, that shall not be thrown down" (Matthew 24:1,2).

According to Jesus, not one stone would be left upon another when the Temple was destroyed. Jesus also predicted the destruction of the city of Jerusalem:

For the days will come upon you, when your enemies will build an embankment around you, surround you and close you in on every side, and level you, and your children within you, to the ground; and they will not leave in you one stone upon another because you did not know the time of your visitation . . .But when you see Jerusalem surrounded by armies, then know that its desolation is near. Then let those in Judea flee to the mountains, let those who are in the midst of her depart, and let not those who are in the country enter her (Luke 19:43,44; 21:20,21).

Daniel's Prediction

The prophet Daniel had also predicted the destruction of the Second Temple:

And after the sixty-two weeks Messiah shall be cut off, but not for Himself; and the people of the prince who is to come shall destroy the city and the sanctuary (Daniel 9:26).

Daniel's prediction said, in effect, that the Messiah would come before Jerusalem and the Temple were destroyed.[11]

Accused of Trying to Destroy the Temple

Jesus was arrested by the religious leaders. One of the charges leveled at Jesus during His trial was that He said He would destroy the Temple:

But at last two false witnesses came forward and said, "This fellow said, 'I am able to destroy the Temple of God and to build it in three days' " (Matthew 26:60,61).

This accusation was based upon an earlier statement made by Jesus:

So the Jews answered and said to Him, "What sign do you show us that you do these things?" Jesus answered and said to them, "Destroy this temple, and in three days I will raise it up." Then the Jews said, "It has taken forty-six years to build this temple and will You raise it up in three days? But He was speaking of the temple of His body. Therefore, when He had risen from the dead, His disciples remembered that He had said this to them; and they believed the Scripture and the word Jesus had said (John 2:18-22).

The Temple Jesus was referring to was not the physical building but rather His body that would be raised from the dead. [12]

Veil of the Temple

Though not found guilty of any crime, Jesus was crucified. Matthew records that, when Jesus died upon the cross, the veil of the Temple was torn :

And behold, the veil of the temple was torn in two from top to bottom; and the earth quaked and the rocks split (Matthew 27:51).

This signified that man now has direct access to God without going through a human priest. The New Testament declares:

There is one God and one Mediator between God and men, the Man Christ Jesus (1 Timothy 2:5).

New Testament References

The references to the Temple in the remainder of the New Testament are few. The Apostle Paul said:

God who made the world and everything in it, since He is Lord of heaven and earth, does not dwell in temples made with hands. Nor is He worshiped with men's hands, as though He needed anything, since He gives to all life, breath, and all things (Acts 17:25,26).

The emphasis is on the New Covenant with the personal presence of Jesus the Messiah dwelling within each individual believer. He is in the midst of His people wherever they go and whenever they gather in His name.

Both Paul and Peter refer to the church as the living Temple:

> Do you not know that you are the temple of God and that the Spirit of God dwells in you? If anyone defiles the temple of God, God will destroy him. For the temple of God is holy, which temple you are . . .Or do you not know that your body is the temple of the Holy Spirit who is in you, whom you have from God, and you are not your own? For you were bought with a price; therefore glorify God in your body and in your spirit, which are God's (1 Corinthians 3:16,17;6:19,20).

> Coming to Him as a living stone, rejected indeed by men, but chosen by God and precious, you also, as living stones, are being built up a spiritual house, a holy priesthood, to offer up spiritual sacrifices acceptable to God through Jesus Christ (1 Peter 2:4,5).

Caligula

Shortly after the death and resurrection of Jesus, the mad Emperor Gaius Julius Caesar Germanicus, nicknamed Caligula ("little boots"), attempted to desecrate the Temple. He gave an order to set up his statue in the Holy of Holies in the Temple. Flavius Josephus wrote:

> Now Caius Caesar did so grossly abuse the fortune he had arrived at, as to take himself to be a god, and to desire to be so called also, and to cut off those of the greatest nobility out of his country. He also extended his impiety as far as the Jews. Accordingly he sent Petronius with an army to Jerusalem to place his statues in the temple, and commanded him that, in case the Jews would not admit of them, he should slay those that opposed it, and carry all the rest into captivity.[13]

The Roman writer Tacitus adds that Caligula commanded the Jews to place his likeness in the Temple. Josephus records that the Jews pleaded with Petronius not to do this. The Jews were willing to sacrifice their whole nation before they would allow the Temple to be defiled. Petronius marveled at their courage and ceased with the process. Thus the confrontation was temporarily averted. An enraged Caligula commanded that Petronius be put to death. Josephus records that Caligula died soon thereafter and due to bad weather at sea, the letter ordering Petronius' death arrived three weeks *after* the news arrived of Caligula's death. Petronius was not executed and the Temple was spared this abomination.

Caligula's attempted act was similar to Antiochus desecrating the Temple in 167 B.C. It seems that God was deferring this act until the end time.

Finally Completed

According to Josephus, the final completion of the Second Temple was not until A.D. 63. The Jews told Jesus that it had taken forty-six years to build the Temple (John 2:19). This probably meant that the workers had already been forty-six years at their task. Herod started the work in 20-18 B.C. and dedicated the Temple in 10 B.C. The work however, was not finished. Josephus tells us that 18,000 builders were still working in A.D. 63 when they were finally dismissed.[14]

Second Temple Destroyed

Seven years after work on the Temple had stopped it was destroyed, The predictions of Jesus were literally fulfilled. Both the Temple and the city of Jerusalem were destroyed. With four Legions, Titus the Roman began a siege of Jerusalem in April, A.D. 70. He posted his 10th legion on the Mount of Olives, directly east of and overlooking the Temple Mount. The 12th and 15th legions were stationed on Mount Scopus, further to the east and commanding all ways to Jerusalem from east to north. The 5th legion was held in reserve.

Titus conferred with his fellow officers as to whether he should destroy the Temple. Though many thought that it would not be a good idea to destroy a structure so magnificent, those who advocated its destruction won out. Roman historian Tacitus reported:

The principal officers were of the opinion that nothing less than the utter destruction of the Temple would secure a lasting peace. A building, which the Jews themselves had made a theatre of blood, ought not, they contended, to be any longer considered a place of worship. It was rather a citadel in which the garrison remained in force . . . and ought to be given up to the fury of an enraged soldiery.

On the 10th of August, in A.D. 70, the 9th of Av in Jewish reckoning, the very day when Nebuchadnezzar burned the Temple in 586 B.C., the Temple was burned again. Titus took the city and put it to the torch.

Jewish historian, Flavius Josephus was present in Jerusalem when the city was captured and the Temple was burnt. He described the event in this manner:

> The Romans, though it was a terrible struggle to collect the timber, raised their platforms in twenty-one days, having, as described before, stripped the whole area in a circle round the town to a distance of ten miles. The countryside like the City was a pitiful sight; for where once there had been a lovely vista of woods and parks there was nothing but desert and stumps of trees. No one—not even a foreigner—who had seen the Old Judea and the glorious suburbs of the City, and now set eyes on her present desolation, could have helped sighing and groaning at so terrible a change; for every trace of beauty had been blotted out by war, and nobody who had known it in the past and came upon it suddenly would have recognized the place: when he was already there he would still have been looking for the City.[15]

Josephus detailed the horrendous outcome:

> To give a detailed account of their outrageous conduct is impossible, but we may sum it up by saying that no other city has ever endured such horrors, and no generation in history has fathered such wickedness. In the end they brought the whole Hebrew race into contempt in order to make their own impiety seem less outrageous in foreign eyes, and confessed the painful truth that they were slaves, the dregs of humanity, bastards, and outcasts of their nation.
>
> . . . It is certain that when from the upper city they watched the Temple burning they did not turn a hair, though many Romans were moved to tears.[16]

The prediction of Jesus with regard to the city and the Temple were now fulfilled:

> As the flames shot into the air the Jews sent up a cry that matched the calamity and dashed to the rescue, with no thought now of saving their lives or husbanding their strength; for that which hitherto they had guarded so devotedly was disappearing before their eyes.[17]

Jerusalem was largely destroyed and, as Jesus had predicted, not one stone was left upon another in the

Temple. As Daniel had predicted, the Temple was
destroyed after the Messiah had come.

Second Exile

When the Temple was destroyed in A.D. 70 the period of
the second exile began. The Jewish people were scattered
throughout the earth. For the next 1900 years the Jews
would have no authority in the land of Palestine. However
during most of the period of this Second Exile there have
been some Jews living in Jerusalem. Although most of the
nation was in exile from their land, the Jews did not forget
Jerusalem or the Temple Mount. Their daily prayer was for
the rebuilding of the Temple in Jerusalem. The traditional
Jewish prayer book contains the following passage:

Because of our sins we were exiled from our country
and banished from our land. We cannot go up as pilgrims
to worship Thee, to perform our duties in Thy chosen
house, the great and Holy Temple which was called by
Thy name, on account of the hand that was let loose on
Thy sanctuary. May it be Thy will, Lord our God and God
of our fathers, merciful King, in Thy abundant love again
to have mercy on us and on Thy sanctuary; rebuild it
speedily and magnify its glory.

Summary

The rise and fall of the two Temples were both predicted
by God. In the ancient world, Jerusalem and its Temple
Mount were center stage to many dramatic events. The
time would come, however, when this area would be
neglected and profaned.

Each of these structures were short-lived. The
Tabernacle was superseded for a permanent structure.
Solomon's Temple was destroyed by the Babylonians,
Zerubbabel's by King Herod, and Herod's by Titus the
Roman. For the next two thousand years, the Temple
Mount would lack any significant Jewish presence.

Endnotes

1.   See our discussion in Appendix 4.

2.   The commandment concerning the "Sabbath year" was given by God in Leviticus 25:1-7. See also Leviticus 26:32-35.

3.   The way biblical critics get around this amazing prophecy is to insist that it was written by a "Second Isaiah" who lived hundreds of years after the fact. Jesus, however, quoted from both sections of Isaiah and attributed it to one author (John 12:38-40).

4.   Josephus, *Antiquities*. Book XI: Chapter 1:2.

5.   How could the Second Temple be more glorious than the First if it were so small in size and without the Ark of the Covenant? The best answer seems to be that the glory of the Second Temple would be the visit of the Messiah.

6.   This purification of the Temple is commemorated every year with the Feast of Hanukah.

7.   The term Hasmonean was used in a broad sense of the entire Maccabean family.

8.   Benjamin Mazar, *The Mountain of the Lord*, New York, Harper and Row, 1975, p. 66.

9.   Actually the Bible speaks of seven different Temples. They are the Tabernacle, Solomon's Temple, Zerubbabel's Temple, Herod's Temple, The Tribulation Temple, Ezekiel's Temple and the heavenly Temple.

10. Why did Jesus use force to cleanse the Temple? See Don Stewart, *What Everyone Needs to Know About Jesus*, Orange, California, Dart Press, 1992.

11.   See our discussion in Appendix 4.

12. Seven times in Scripture the body of Christ is referred to as the Temple of God. They are found in 1 Corinthians 3:16,17; 6:19, 2 Corinthians 6:16, Ephesians 2:21, Hebrews 3:6, 1 Peter 2:5; 4:17.

13. Josephus, *Antiquities* 2:20.

14. Josephus, *Wars of the Jews*, Book 5, Chapter 4:2.

15. Josephus, *Wars of the Jews*, Book 5, Chapter 4:4.

16. Josephus, *Wars of the Jews*, Book 5, Chapter 10:5.

17. Josephus, *Wars of the Jews*, Book 6, Chapter 5:1.

CHAPTER FOUR

JERUSALEM LOST: THE TEMPLE MOUNT PROFANED

> Ten parts of beauty were allotted the world at large, and of
> these Jerusalem assumed nine measures and the rest of
> the world but one . . . ten parts of suffering were visited
> upon the world—nine for Jerusalem and one for the
> world—The Jewish sages

The destruction of the Temple in A.D. 70 caused the
beginning of the scattering of the Jews throughout the
world. During this period, the Temple Mount was for the
most part neglected and profaned. Though this time
constituted a period of neglect some significant events
concerning Jerusalem and the Temple Mount did occur.

Hadrian

In the first hundred years after the city and Temple
were destroyed, there was high expectation among the
Jews that they would once again return to their land and
rebuild that which had been devastated. The Court of 70
Elders, the Sanhedrin, was intact and many Jews still
lived in small communities in Israel. There is some evidence
that Hadrian (A.D. 118-135) gave the Jews permission to
rebuild their Temple early in his reign.

The Jewish Encyclopedia writes:

> It appears that Hadrian already granted permission
> for the rebuilding of the Temple; that the Jews of the
> diaspora had already begun to return to Jerusalem, and
> that the brothers Pappus and Julian had already
> provided for the exchange of foreign money into Roman
> coin . . . Of the intended rebuilding of the Temple under
> Hadrian mention is made by Chrysostom (Orat. iii. in
> Judaeos"), "Chron. Alex." (on the year 118), Nicephorus
> (Hist. Ecc." iii. 24), and Cedrenus (Script. Byz. xii. 249).[1]

Hadrian seems to have requested that the site of the new Temple be different from its former location. This was, of course, unsatisfactory to the Jews. Whether the rebuilding process was actually started during the early years of Hadrian's reign is uncertain.

The Jewish hopes were later dashed when Hadrian decided to establish a new city on the ruins of Jerusalem. The Old City was plowed up to make way for the new Roman city to be named Colonia Aelia Capitolina.

Second Jewish Revolt

The Jews then rebelled against the Romans. In response, there were large scale mass murders of Jews in Caesarea and other communities. The murders sparked a larger rebellion led by a man named Bar Kochba (A.D. 132-135). Bar Kochba rallied the people and massacred the famous 12th legion of the Roman army. Jerusalem was liberated for three years and Rabbi Akiva proclaimed Bar Kochba as the Messiah who was to deliver the Jewish people.

The Jews set up an independent government. Coins were struck that commemorated the "First Year of the Deliverance of Israel." Another coin that was struck showed the facade of the Temple.

Within three years of Jerusalem's liberation, Rome marched against the rebels and killed Bar Kochba. The Sanhedrin labeled him a false Messiah and Jerusalem was again in Roman hands. Jewish Jerusalem was blotted out and Aelia Capitolina was built on its site. Because the war had cost the lives of Roman heroes, the Jews were forbidden to enter Jerusalem upon penalty of death. Hadrian attempted to destroy every connection Jerusalem had with the Jewish people.

It is probable that attempts were made to rebuild the Temple during the period of A.D. 132-135. One later historical work called *Chronicon Paschale* describes Hadrian as the one who destroyed the Temple of the Jews. The Roman historian Dio Cassius also said that Hadrian built his Temple to replace the one of the God of Israel. Some, therefore, assume that the *Chronicon* is not referring to the destruction of the original Temple by Titus in A.D. 70 but to a later destruction by Hadrian of a partially restored Temple built by Bar Kochba.

In an effort to leave no trace of the Temple, Hadrian erected a Temple to Jupiter Capitolinus on the Temple Mount. An equestrian statue of Hadrian was also built in front of it. A small temple to Venus was also built (the present site of the church of the Holy Sepulchre).

The next Emperor, Antonius Pius (A.D. 138-161) added another statue. The Jews were only allowed to enter the city on special occasions to mourn on the Temple Mount.[2]

Constantine

Emperor Constantine and his mother Queen Helen were converted to Christianity. In A.D. 324 Aelia Capitolina was renamed Jerusalem and the title of "Holy City" was restored to her. It was now, however, considered the Holy City of Christianity. The pagan temple of Jupiter was destroyed and the church of Holy Zion was built upon the Temple Mount. These conditions lasted until A.D. 362 when the Roman emperor Julian the Apostate permitted the Jews to return.

A Plan to Rebuild

There was only one other occasion since the destruction of the Second Temple that serious plans were made to rebuild. The person behind this project was the Roman Emperor, Flavius Claudius Julianus, a nephew of Constantine. He was also known as Julian the Apostate because of his opposition to Christianity. Julian planned the project in the last year of his reign in A.D. 363. Julian rescinded all the anti-Jewish laws that his uncle Constantine had instituted. He issued an edict that the Temple be rebuilt in Jerusalem. This caused a great deal of excitement among the Jews. From far and wide, Jews came to Jerusalem to help in the rebuilding work. Julian supplied the necessary funds and appointed Alypius of Antioch, Governor of Great Britain, to carry out the project. Jews from all over gave from their wealth upon the projected work of rebuilding the Temple. The roads to Jerusalem were filled with multitudes of Jewish men and women who had hopes of seeing a Third Temple built.

Hopes are Dashed

However tragedy struck. The foundations were barely uncovered when flames of fire burst forth from under the ground. The flames were accompanied by large explosions.

The workmen fled and the building was stopped, never again to be restarted. A massive earthquake had struck Jerusalem. Philip C. Hammond explains what happened:

The stones were piled and ready. Costly wood had been purchased. The necessary metal was at hand. The Jews of Jerusalem were rejoicing. Tomorrow—May 20, 363 A.D.– the rebuilding of the Temple would begin! Almost 200 years after the Roman Legions under Titus had destroyed the Temple, the Emperor Julian—called by his Christian subjects "the Apostate"—had given his imperial permission to rebuild the Temple. The Jewish people eagerly responded. . .

Suddenly, and without warning, at the third hour of the night (the third hour after sunset according to Roman practice) the streets of Jerusalem trembled and buckled, crushing two hundred years of hope in a pile of dust. No longer would there be any possibility of rebuilding the Temple.[3]

There are those who believed that the earthquake was a demonstration of the anger of God. With their hopes dashed, the Jews were then driven into Exile and became wanderers in foreign lands. They were people without a homeland. For some eighteen centuries they would be dispersed and persecuted. Throughout time their thoughts were of the Temple which once stood in Jerusalem and their prayers for its restoration.

Visible Remains

From ancient records we can derive some information about visible remains of the Temple after its destruction.

Eusebius, bishop of Caesarea, (A.D. 260-340) testified that he could still see the remains of the sanctuary. He said that the large stone blocks were hauled away to build sanctuaries and theaters.

During this period of exile the city was visited by a pilgrim known as the traveler of Bordeaux. He gave the following testimony in A.D. 333:

At the side of the Sanctuary, there is a pierced stone. Jews visit there once a year, pour oil over it, lament and weep over it, and tear their garments in token of mourning. Then they return home.

The once a year visit was on the 9th of Av, the Jewish date of the destruction of both Temples. The pierced stone, or a rock with a hollow in it, is not identified. It is assumed to be the foundation stone upon which the Holy of Holies was built. In the Talmud we find a reference to the

"Foundation Rock" upon which the Holy of Holies had rested (Yoma 5:2).

Early church father Chrysostom wrote:

> The Jews began uncovering the foundations by removing masses of earth, intending to go ahead and build . . . You can see the bared foundations if you visit Jerusalem now. . . Some of its parts (sanctuary) are razed to the ground.

In A.D. 392, the Christian leader Jerome wrote about the Jew's practice on the anniversary of the Temple's destruction:

> On the anniversary of the day when the city fell and was destroyed by the Romans, there are crowds who mourn, old women and old men dressed in tatters and rags, and from the top of the Mount of Olives this throng laments over the destruction of its Sanctuary. Still their eyes flow with tears, still their hands tremble and their hair is dishevelled, but already the guards demand pay for their right to weep.[4]

In the sixth century the Pilgrim of Piacenze mentions the ruins of the Temple of Solomon.

From these accounts we can deduce that there were at least some visible remains of the Temple through the sixth century.

Cursed of God

In the early years, the Christians looked upon the Temple Mount as a place that God had cursed. As Christianity gained foothold in the Roman world the Temple Mount was left to become a desolate rubble heap.

In A.D. 534, over the site of Solomon's elaborate palace, the Emperor Justinian built mighty substructures as foundations for the New Church of St. Mary. While other holy sites in Jerusalem were explored and identified, the Temple Mount was neglected.

Anti-Semitism

One of the greatest tragedies of history was the anti-Semitism that arose among the "Christians" during this period. Concerning the Jews, early Christian leader John Chrysostom falsely wrote:

They sacrificed their sons and daughters to devils: they outraged nature and overthrew their foundations the laws of relationship. They are become worse than the wild beasts, and for no reason at all, with their own hands, they murder their offspring, to worship the avenging devils who are foes of our life . . . They know only one thing, to satisfy their gullets, get drunk, to kill and maim one another.[5]

Chrysostom delivered eight sermons which expressed intense hatred of the Jews. His accusations were nothing but outright lies. The purpose of these falsehoods was to keep the Christians in Antioch from having any contact with the Jews.

In another act of anti-Semitism, Bishop Ambrose of Milan ordered a synagogue to be set on fire. When Emperor Theodosius demanded an explanation, the Bishop wrote him back:

I declare that I have set fire to the synagogue, or at least that those who did acted on my orders, so that there would be no place where Christ is rejected . . . Moreover, the synagogue was in fact destroyed by the judgment of God.[6]

This desecration even angered the Romans. The bishop was required to rebuild the synagogue and those who had participated in its destruction were punished.

These and others failed to realize that it was God who scattered the Jewish people and that He had ultimate purposes in doing so. The Jews would be a blessing to each city in which they were scattered, to be regathered by God at the right time.

With the Jews scattered, Jerusalem was about to be conquered by a new religion—one that would have prominence for the next 1,300 years. That religion was Islam.

Endnotes

1.   Encyclopedia Judaica, Vol 1, p. 213.

2.   This episode may have future implications that are just now being recognized. See our comments in Chapter Ten.

3.   Philip C. Hammond, "New Light on the Nabataens," *Biblical Archaeological Review*, March/April 1981, p. 23.

4.   Jerome's commentary on Isaiah 2:9.

5.   Chrysostom's Sermons, cited by J. Parkes, *The Conflict of the Church and the Synagogue*, pp. 105-106.

6.   Bishop Ambrose, "Eleventh Letter to Theodosius," as quoted by Parkes, ibid. pp. 163-164.

CHAPTER FIVE

ENTER ISLAM

In the 7th Century A.D. a new religion burst upon the scene, Islam. Soon after its beginning, Islam conquered Jerusalem and took control of the Temple Mount. Historian Steve Runciman recounts the incident:

> On a February day in the year A.D. 638 the Caliph Omar entered Jerusalem, riding upon a white camel. He was dressed in worn, filthy robes, and the army that followed him was rough and unkempt; but its discipline was perfect. At his side was the Patriarch Sophronius, as chief magistrate of the surrendered city. Omar rode straight to the site of the Temple of Solomon, whence his friend Mahomet had ascended into heaven. Watching him stand there, the Patriarch remembered the words of Christ and murmured through his tears: 'Behold the abomination of desolation, spoken of by Daniel the prophet.'[1]

Omar was shocked at the filth and rubble that lay strewn about the Temple Mount. Because the holy site had been neglected he made the Christian Patriarch Sophronius grovel in the muck. Afterward Omar set about clearing the site. He then built a wooden mosque on the Temple Mount.

Islam and the Temple Mount

Since it is a historical fact that Mohammed never came to Jerusalem, why is the Temple Mount considered holy to Moslems? There is a passage from the Koran that links Mohammed with Jerusalem and the Temple Mount. It is in the seventeenth Sura, "The Night Journey." In it there is a dream or vision by Mohammed in which he is carried by night:

> . . . from the sacred temple to the temple that is more remote, whose precinct we have blessed, that we might show him of our signs.[2]

Islamic tradition identifies the first temple as Mecca and the second as Jerusalem. Mohammed's journey was with the Archangel Gabriel. Moslem belief says they rode together on a winged steed called El Burak ("lightning"). El Burak is not mentioned in the Koran; its first mention is two centuries after Mohammed's death in a document called *Hadith*, a collection of oral traditions.

After they arrived at the Temple Mount they ascended through the seven heavens into Allah's presence. Various spots on the Mount were later indicated as the place where El Burak was tied up before the ascent into the presence of Allah. A later account of the night journey states:

The prophet of God said: 'While I was sleeping within the wall of the Kaaba, came to see me Gabriel and kicked me with his foot, so I sat up, but not seeing anything, I lay again on my bed. He kicked me then once more, and I sat up and did not see a thing, so I lay back on my bed. He then kicked me a third time and I sat up, whereupon he pulled me by the arm and I rose, and went to the door of the temple. There was standing a white beast, between a mule and an ass in size, with two wings on its thighs, digging its hind legs in and placing its forelegs as far as it can see. Gabriel carried me on the beast, and we went together at the same speed.' So the Prophet of God journeyed, and with him also Gabriel, until they reached the temple in Jerusalem. He found there Abraham, Moses and Jesus, among other prophets, and he led them in prayers. Then he was given two vessels, one filled with wine and the other with milk, so the prophet of God took the vessel with milk and drank it, leaving the vessel of wine. Seeing that, Gabriel said to him: 'You were guided to the true religion [Islam] and so was your nation, for wine is forbidden unto you.'

The Dome of the Rock

In A.D. 691 Caliph Abd El-Malik commissioned the best architects to build the Dome of the Rock. It was based upon a sixth century octagonal Byzantine church in Mt. Gerizim. The shrine was built as a political, economic, and religious counter attraction to Mecca. Medina and Mecca, the two cities holy to Islam, were under the control of a rival Caliph. Abd El-Malik wanted to build up the importance of Jerusalem as an Islamic center for pilgrimage and worship. The holy spot of Judaism was now identified with the spot where Mohammed's horse ascended to heaven.

There is, however, no convincing evidence that the Dome of the Rock was purposely built over the site of the First and Second Temples. It is possible that they were built over Roman ruins of the temple of Jupiter.[3]

Although Abd El-Malik had commissioned the structure, it became known as "The Mosque of Omar." The structure, however, is not a mosque but rather a shrine.

Inside the Dome is the "Sacred Rock." On the rock's surface is an indentation which is believed by Moslems, to be the footprint left by Mohammed as he leapt into heaven. The same rock is the traditional site of Abraham's sacrificial altar for Isaac, and the site of the First and Second Temple. The Crusaders were known to chip "holy souvenirs" from it.

East of the rock is a tall cupboard where it is believed hairs from the beard of Mohammed are contained. Within the hollowed out chamber of the rock are the "places of prayer" of Elijah, Abraham, David, and Solomon. The Moslems call this cave the "well of souls" where they believe the dead meet twice a week to pray.

The outside of the Dome is covered with tiles from Persia as well as marble. The "Golden Dome" is not made out of gold but rather anodized aluminum. There are about forty-five thousand tiles used in the Dome and on its outer walls. Most of them were installed later by Suleiman the Magnificent (A.D. 1517).

During the seventeen centuries of the Dome's existence it has undergone many repairs, but it has not been substantially changed since its completion in A.D 691. After one of the earliest renovations in A.D 820, Caliph al-Mamun took off the name of Caliph Abd el-Malik from the dedication plate and inserted his own name instead. However he neglected to change the dates and his fraud is there for all to see.

In medieval times this spot was considered to be the "center of the world" and was marked such on various maps.

The Dome's Beauty

Writing about A.D 985, Mukadassi, the famous Moslem traveler born in Jerusalem, wrote:

> At the dawn, when the light of the sun first strikes on the cupola and the drum catches the rays, then is this edifice a marvelous site to behold and one such that in all Islam I have never seen its equal; neither have I heard tell

of aught built in pagan times that could rival in grace this Dome of the Rock.

Denial of Christianity

From the Moslem point of view the Dome of the Rock was an answer to, and a denial of, the attractions of Christianity and its Scriptures, providing the "faithful" with arguments to be used against Christian theology. The inscriptions on its walls are seven hundred and thirty-four feet long in all, amongst the lengthiest inscriptions in the world. There is a great amount of repetition and many quotations from the Koran.

The following extracts are relevant:

Inner Face

South Wall. In the name of Allah the Merciful the Compassionate. There is no God but Allah alone; he has no co-partner. He is the Kingship and His the praise. He giveth life and He causeth to die, and He hath power over everything.

South-East Wall. Verily Allah and His angels pronounce blessing upon the Prophet. O ye who have pronounced blessings upon Him and give Him the salutation of peace. O, People of the Book (i.e. the Jews and Christians, always referred to as such by the Moslems) do not go beyond the bounds in your religion and do not say about Allah anything but the truth. The Messiah, Jesus, son of Mary, is but a messenger of Allah and His word which he cast upon Mary, and a spirit from Him. So believe only in Allah and of his messenger, but do not say "Three" (Trinity) and it will be better for you. Allah is only one God. Far be it from His glory that he should have a son.

North Wall. The Messiah will not deign to be in the service of Allah nor will the angels who stand in his presence. O Allah; pray upon Thy messenger "the servant Jesus—*(N-W Wall)* — the son of Mary and peace be upon him the day of his birth, the day of his death and the day of his being raised alive." That is Jesus, son of Mary—a statement concerning which YOU are in doubt. It is not for Allah to take for Himself any offspring, glory be to Him.

West Wall. Allah bears witness that there is no God but Him, likewise the angels and the people possessed of knowledge *(S-W WALL)*— Upholding justice. There is no God but He, the Almighty and All wise. Verily, the religion in Allah's sight is Islam.

Outer Face

West and North-West Walls. In the name of Allah the
Merciful and Compassionate. There is no God but Allah
alone. Praise be to Allah who hath not taken to himself
offspring. To Him there has never been any person in the
sovereignty. Mohammed is the messenger of Allah, may
God pray upon Him and accept his intercession.

Praise be God who has not taken unto himself a son
and who has no partner in sovereignty nor has He any
protector on account of weakness.

One will observe from the sayings on the wall that they
are blasphemies against Jesus Christ.

Al Aqsa Mosque

Al Aqsa is mentioned in the Koran in a vision of
Mohammad's Ascension. It means the "distant place."
This refers to its geographical location far from Mecca. It is
Islam's third holiest shrine after Mecca and Medina. The
present mosque is believed to stand over the area where
Solomon built his magnificent palace south of the Temple.

The Al Aqsa Mosque was built between A.D. 709-715 by
Caliph Waleed, son of Abd el-Malik, who constructed the
Dome of the Rock. Throughout the years the mosque has
been destroyed several times by earthquakes and
subsequently rebuilt. A few supporting columns east of the
cupola are the most prominent remains of the original
mosque that has survived.

The most important reconstruction was after an
earthquake in A.D 1034 when the mosque was enlarged to
seat 5000 worshipers. The builders used capitals and
columns of destroyed Byzantine churches in their
reconstruction.

Jewish Hopes

The conquering Moslems brought a different attitude
with them. In contrast to the Byzantine and Roman
conquerors who let the Temple Mount remain in ruins as a
proof of the destruction of Jewish nationalism, the
Moslems restored worship to the Mount. Yet the worship
was not of Yahweh, the God of the Bible, but of Allah.

When the Moslems became the rulers in Jerusalem
things became easier for the Jews. They were officially
allowed to live in the city and there is evidence that on

certain holy days they were permitted on the Temple Mount.

Reports say that the Jews would march in procession around the walls of the Temple Mount on feast days and pray at the gates. A document written in the tenth century indicates that one of the conditions for allowing the Jews to pray at the gates was that the Jewish community would be responsible for keeping the Mount clean. The Jews, it states, were responsible to sweep the Mount. Other accounts indicate that Jews were employed in the Mosque area and that Jewish craftsmen made lamps for the Mosque.

Inscriptions have been found at the gates of the Temple Mount that were probably put there by Jewish Pilgrims during the early Arab rule. One such inscription, when translated, reads:

> You Lord of Hosts build this House in the lifetime of Jacob ben-Jospeh, Theophylactus, and Sisinia and Anistasia. Amen and amen.

The names on the inscription indicate they were Jews from a Greek-speaking country. Though the Jews were allowed more access than in the Roman or Byzantine period, they were still far from their desired goal of retaking Jerusalem and the Temple Mount.

Crusaders Capture Jerusalem

In the last 1300 years, with only one exception, the Temple Mount has been in the hands of Moslems. On July 15, 1099 Jerusalem was taken from the Moslems by the Crusaders from Europe. The Crusaders slaughtered the inhabitants of Jerusalem in an unjustified carnage. The Dome of the Rock was converted into a Christian Church called the *Templum Domini*—Temple of our Lord.

The Al Aqsa Mosque was used as headquarters of the Knights of the Templar who officiated the Temple Compound. A remnant of the Crusader occupation still exists, the tombs of the assassins of Thomas Beckett, the Archbishop of Canterbury (1118-1170). After murdering Beckett, the assassins traveled to Jerusalem and took up with the Templar Knights. Their tombs are situated near the main entrance.

The Western world rejoiced that Jerusalem was in the hands of "Christians." The victory, however, caused the

Moslems to immediately launch campaigns to regain the city and the Dome from the Christian infidels.

Saladin

The Crusader occupation was relatively short-lived. The Moslem leader Saladin (Salah ad-Din) proclaimed a *jihad* or holy war to retake the land of Palestine. After ninety years of Crusader control, Jerusalem surrendered to Saladin's army on October 2, 1187. In contrast to the brutality of the Crusaders, Saladin treated the defeated Crusaders with kindness and mercy.

The golden cross that had been placed on the Dome of the Rock was torn down. Saladin rededicated the Templar's headquarters as a mosque. The Dome was covered with beautiful mosaics and a prayer niche facing Mecca was added.

Jerusalem was back in the hands of the Moslems and Europe was ready to avenge the defeat. A Third Crusade was undertaken (1189-1192) to free Jerusalem from the armies of Saladin. Richard the Lion-hearted led England and other Crusaders in a fruitless attempt to retake the city. To this day, the Temple Mount remains in Moslem control.

Jerusalem Desolate

In 1267 the Jewish sage Nahmanides wrote a letter to his son. It contained the following references to the land and the Temple:

> What shall I say of this land . . . The more holy the place the greater the desolation. Jerusalem is the most desolate of all . . . There are about 2,000 inhabitants . . . but there are no Jews, for after the arrival of the Tartars, the Jews fled, and some were killed by the sword. There are now only two brothers, dyers, who buy their dyes from the government. At their place a quorum of worshippers meets on the Sabbath, and we encourage them, and found a ruined house, built on pillars, with a beautiful dome, and made it into a synagogue . . . People regularly come to Jerusalem, men and women from Damascus and from Aleppo and from all parts of the country, to see the Temple and weep over it. And may He who deemed us worthy to see Jerusalem in her ruins, grant us to see her rebuilt and restored, and the honor of the Divine Presence returned.

The Mishna shows the reverence that was required of the Jews for the Temple site:

> No man shall behave frivolously when standing near the eastern gate, which looks to the Holy of Holies; he shall not enter the Temple Mount with his cane, his shoes, his purse or the dust on his feet, nor shall he use it as a short cut, still less shall he spit there.[4]

Turkish Rule

The Ottoman Turks, non-Arab Moslems, became the dominant power in the 15th century. In 1453 they captured the city of Constantinople and brought about the final destruction of the Eastern Roman Empire (Byzantine). They renamed the city Istanbul and made it the center of their empire.

In 1517, under Sultan Selim I, the Turks captured Jerusalem and all of Israel. The rule of the Turks over Jerusalem would last exactly 400 years. The walls which today surround the Old City were built by Suleiman the Magnificent, son of Sultan Selim. Suleiman restored the Al Aqsa Mosque and some of the present stained glass windows date from this period.

The Arabs found themselves under the domination of the Turks. For 400 years of Turkish rule the Arabs did not have one independent state.

Napoleon

There is an account of Napoleon visiting the Temple Mount on the 9th of Av, the day of the commemoration of the Temple's destruction. When asked what all the crying and wailing was about he was told that the Jews were mourning their Temple which had been destroyed 1800 years previously. Touched by the incident Napoleon said, "a people which weeps and mourns for the loss of its homeland 1800 years ago and does not forget-such a people will never be destroyed. Such a people can rest assured that its homeland will be returned to it."

The hope of the captives in Exile is that one day they would again come to their land, rebuild the Holy City and their Temple.

Non-Moslems Barred

J.T. Barclay in the mid 19th Century wrote about the barring of those from the Mount who were not of the Islamic faith:

> When the clock of the Mosk needs repairing, they are compelled, however reluctantly, to employ a Frank. But in order to have a clean conscience in the commission of such an abominable piece of sacrilege as the admission upon the sacred premises, they adopt the following expedient. The mechanic selected being thoroughly purged from his uncleanness ablution . . . a certain formula of prayer and incantation is sung over him at the gate. This being satisfactorily concluded, he is considered as exorcized, not only of Christianity (or Judaism, as the case may be), but of humanity also; and is declared to be no longer a man but a donkey. He is then mounted upon the shoulders of the faithful, lest . . . the ground should be polluted by his footsteps; and being carried to the spot where his labours are required, he is set down upon matting within certain prescribed limits; and the operation being performed, he is carried back to the gate, and there by certain other ceremonies, he is duly *undonkeyfied* and transmuted back into a man again.[5]

Palestinian Exploration Society

In 1867 to 1870, under the auspices of the Palestinian Exploration Society, British engineer Charles Warren conducted a series of excavations around the outer wall of the Temple area. It was the first scientific study ever performed on the Temple area. Warren's work was heroic considering the dreadful conditions in which he had to work. No further scientific work would be done on the Temple Mount for another one hundred years.

Jewish Persecution

Toward the end of the nineteenth century, Jewish persecution was on the increase. In 1882, as a result of persecution of the Jews in Russia and Romania, the first immigration of Jewish settlers to Palestine began.

In 1891 Arab leaders prepared a petition to the Ottoman government in Constantinople to demand an end to Jewish immigration into Palestine and to prohibit Jewish land purchases.

In 1896 Theodor Herzl, the founder of modern Zionism, published the *Jewish State*. He argued that the only way in which the "Jewish problem" can be resolved was by establishing a Jewish state in Palestine. Herzl's writings started the Jews on the road back to their Promised homeland.

Parker Expedition

During this period of Turkish rule, one of the biggest uproars that ever occurred around the Temple Mount happened at the beginning of this century—the ill-fated Parker expedition. Captain Montague Parker organized an expedition to Jerusalem to find a $200 million treasure that was supposedly hidden underneath the Temple. A Swedish philosopher named Valter H. Juvelius thought he found a coded passage in the book of Ezekiel that gave the location of this lost treasure. Since digging was not allowed on the Temple Mount, Parker and his group had to content themselves with digging around the area. After months of digging around the Temple Mount, no "secret passage" could be found. With their permit to dig about to expire Parker bribed the Turkish governor to let him and his cohorts secretly dig on the Temple Mount. Dressed in Arab garb, the group came to the Mount at night and stealthily dug while it was dark. For about a week they continued this practice. However just when they began to excavate the place where they believed the treasure to be, fate intervened. An attendant of the Mosque decided to sleep that night on the Temple Mount. Hearing strange noises coming from the Mosque he decided to investigate. He came upon Parker and his illegal dig. Immediately the horrified Moslem took to the streets to reveal this sacrilege. The result was a riot:

> On the morning of April 19, 1911, a crowd of angry Moslems, outraged at what they considered to be a desecration of the holy Mosque of Omar or the Dome of the Rock, rampaged through the streets of Jerusalem, quickly mobbing the entrance to the government citadel. The Turkish governor of the city, fearing for his own life at the hands of the crowd, ordered troops to quell the disturbance. But the soldiers were unable to control the growing mobs, and by nightfall, rioting and mayhem had spread to all parts of the city.
> Never before had an archaeological expedition ended in so violent an uproar. But never before had there been an archaeological expedition quite like Captain Parker's.

Conceived in folly, but planned with cunning, the Parker Mission had come to Jerusalem with a single goal: to locate and unearth the fantastic treasure of Solomon's Temple buried beneath the Temple Mount.[6]

Parker and his companions escaped with their lives but the episode is another of the strange events that have occurred around the Temple and the Temple Mount.

World War I

When the first World War occurred the Arabs helped the British fight the Turks. D.E. Lawrence, "Lawrence of Arabia," was instrumental in achieving the victory over the Ottoman Empire.

In October 1917 General Allenby launched an invasion in the land of Palestine. On Sunday, December 9th, the Turks were driven out of Jerusalem. Two days later the General made his entry into conquered Jerusalem on foot. He said no one could enter the Holy City except in humility on foot. He said upon entering:

Since your city is regarded with affection by the adherents of three great religions of mankind, and its soil has been consecrated by the prayers and the pilgrimages of devout people of these three religions for many centuries, therefore I do make known to you . . . that all sacred buildings will be maintained and protected according to the existing customs and beliefs of those whose faiths are sacred.

Britain, France and Russia forged the Sykes-Picot Agreement which carved up the Ottoman Empire following its defeat in World War I. Britain gained control of Palestine. For the first time in 400 years the Holy sites of Christianity were delivered from the domination of Islam.

Balfour Declaration

On November 2, 1917 the British government, in the Balfour declaration, pledged its support for a nation home in Palestine for the Jews. British Foreign Secretary Lord Balfour wrote a letter to Baron Edward de Rothchild as a representative of the Jewish people:

His majesty's Government view with favour the establishment in Palestine of a national home for the Jewish people, and will use their best endeavors to facilitate the achievement of this objective, it being clearly understood that nothing shall be done which may prejudice the civil and religious rights of existing and non-Jewish communities in Palestine, or the rights and political status enjoyed by Jews in any other country.[7]

The Arabs believed they had been betrayed. Because the Arabs had helped the British oust the Turks they expected to receive full control of Palestine. Britain said that Arab independence did not include the land of Palestine.[8]

The situation was bad for both Jews and Arabs. The Turks were no longer in control, it was now the British who were their new masters.

Riots of 1929

The land of Palestine saw riots occur in 1929. Agents of the Grand Mufti began spreading false rumors among the Palestinian Arabs that the Jews planned to attack the Dome of the Rock. An armed Arab mob, inflamed by these claims, descended upon the Jewish part of Jerusalem on August 23. During the following week the violence spread throughout the entire country. By the time British reinforcement arrived, 133 Jews had been killed as well as 116 Arabs. This outbreak had an important impact on British policy concerning the Holy Land. Again the Temple Mount was at the center of the controversy.

As we have already observed, history has provided many examples of anti-Semitism among "Christians." Yet there are many examples of others who helped the Jews. One Christian who made a significant contribution toward the rebirth of the State of Israel was Orde Wingate.

From 1936-1939 the Arabs of Palestine revolted in an attempt to halt the establishment of a Jewish homeland in Palestine. British army units as well as Jewish settlements came under attack.

Captain Wingate, a Bible-believing Christian, was posted as an intelligence officer to Jerusalem in 1936. At the time of his arrival, a new wave or terrorism had broken out among the settlements.

To counter this terrorism, Wingate trained special units that helped defend against the Arab attacks. He introduced successful techniques in countering the marauding bands. His heroic efforts did much to insure the security of the Jewish settlers.

Wingate explained why he felt responsible to help the Jewish people:

This is the cause of your survival. I count it as my privilege to help you fight your battle. To that purpose I want to devote my life. I believe that the very existence of mankind is justified when it is based on the moral foundation of the Bible. Whoever dares lift a hand against you and your enterprise here should be fought against. Whether it is jealously, ignorance or perverted doctrine, such as have made your neighbors rise against you, or "politics" which make some of my countrymen support them, I shall fight with you against any of these influences. But remember that it is your battle. My part, which I say I feel to be a privilege, is only to help you.[9]

The example of Orde Wingate serves as a reminder that those who accept the Bible literally cannot help but have a love for God's chosen people, the Jews. Wingate's story is in contrast to the unspeakable things said and done in the past by those who claimed they were doing it in the name of Christ. To those individuals who persecuted the Jews, desecrated the Temple Mount and other Jewish Holy Places, all in the name of Christianity, Jesus said, "I never knew you; depart from Me, you who practice lawlessness!" (Matthew 7:23).

United Nations Partition

The British finally gave up and turned the problem of Palestine over to the United Nations. The United Nations voted to partition the land of Palestine into two states: one for the Palestinian Arabs and the other for the Jews. War was inevitable.

The British mandate was set to end on May 15, 1948. The Arab leaders promised they would invade Palestine at that date and crush the Jews. Poised on the border were the armies of Egypt, Syria and Iraq. They were ready to deliver the death blow to the newly formed state. The Jordanian army already held strategic positions within Palestine. The Jews had no planes, tanks or artillery to handle a full-scale invasion. Furthermore, there was no place for them to retreat. Everything looked hopeless.

May 14, 1948—Israel Receives Statehood

On May 14, 1948, against all the odds, the modern state of Israel was reborn. At four o'clock that afternoon the members of the provisional national council, led by David Ben-Gurion, met in the Tel Aviv Art Museum. Ben-

Gurion rose and read the following proclamation to the assembled guests:

The Land of Israel was the birthplace of the Jewish people. Here their spiritual, religious and national identity was formed. Here they achieved independence and created a culture of national and universal significance. Here they wrote and gave the Bible to the world.

Exiled from Palestine, the Jewish people remained, faithful to it in all countries of their dispersion, never ceasing to pray and hope for their return and the restoration of their national freedom. . .

Accordingly we, the members of the National Council, representing the Jewish people in Palestine and the Zionist movement of the world, met together in solemn assembly today, the day of the termination of the British Mandate of Palestine, by virtue of the natural and historic right of the Jewish people and the Resolution of the General Assembly of the United Nations, hereby proclaim the establishment of the Jewish state in Palestine, to be called ISRAEL . . .

With trust in Almighty God, we set our hand to this declaration, at this session of the Provisional State Council, in the city of Tel Aviv, on this Sabbath eve, the fifth year of Iyar, 5708, the fourteenth day of May, 1948.

War of Independence

As promised the new state of Israel was attacked by Arab forces as soon as their independence was declared. The result was an amazing victory for Israel and a staggering defeat for their Arab enemies. Jews started to return to Israel. *Time* magazine reported:

Out of the concentration camps, ghettos, courtrooms, theatres and factories of Europe the Chosen People had assembled and won their first great military victory since 166-160 B.C. Israel's victory came after the worst of a thousand persecutions.[10]

The Bible had predicted the Lord would scatter His people:

Then the Lord will scatter you among all peoples, from one end of the earth to the other, and there you shall serve other gods, which neither you nor your fathers have known—wood and stone. And among those nations you shall find no rest, nor shall the sole of your foot have a resting place; but there the Lord will give you a trembling heart, failing eyes, and anguish of soul (Deuteronomy 28:64-66).

Scripture also had predicted He would bring them back:

Now it shall come to pass, when all these things come upon you, the blessing and the curse which I have set before you, and you call them to mind among the nations where the Lord your God drives, you, and you will return to the Lord your God and obey His voice, according to all that I commanded you today, you and your children, with all your heart and with all your soul, that the Lord will bring you back from captivity, and have compassion on you, and gather you again from all the nations where the Lord God has scattered you (Deuteronomy 30:1-3).[11]

Now they were back, but not totally. The Jews did not control the Temple Mount area or the Old City of Jerusalem. In 1948 full Moslem control of the Old City of Jerusalem, including the Temple Mount returned to Islamic rule when King Abdullah took that part of the city in the War of Independence.

King Assassinated

The Temple Mount remained in the headlines. On Friday June 13, 1951 King Abdullah of Transjordan was assassinated at the entrance of the Al Aqsa Mosque. A bullet scarred pillar just inside the entrance serves as a reminder of the event.

One of the bullets deflected and almost killed his grandson, the present ruler of Jordan, King Hussein. King Hussein took over his rule at the age of seventeen. He was the first person to fully lift restrictions to non-Moslems to visit the Enclosures and the interior of the Dome of the Rock and the Al Aqsa Mosque.

From 1948 to 1967, Jerusalem was a divided city with tensions running high on both sides. It was only a matter of time until the city would experience another war for total control.

Summary

From the time of the destruction of the Second Temple until June 1967, the city, except for three short years under Bar Kochba, had never been in Jewish control. The

story of the Jews is one of wandering and humiliation. Yet
they came back and the modern state of Israel was reborn.
Mark Twain wrote:

> If the statistics are right, the Jews constitute but one
> per cent of the human race. It suggests a nebulous dim
> puff of star dust lost in the blaze of the Milky Way.
> Properly the Jew ought hardly to be heard of; but he is
> heard of. He is as prominent on the planet as any other
> people, and his commercial importance is extravagantly
> out of proportion to the smallness of his bulk. His
> contributions to the world's list of great names in
> literature, science, art, music, finance, medicine . . . are
> also way out of proportion to the weakness of his
> numbers. He has made a marvelous fight in this world, in
> all the ages; and has done it with his hands tied behind
> him. He could be vain of himself, and be excused for it. The
> Egyptian, the Babylonian and the Persian rose, filled the
> planet with sound and splendour, then faded to dream-
> stuff and passed away; the Greek and the Roman
> followed, and made a vast noise, and they are gone; other
> peoples have sprung up and held their torch high for a
> time, but it burned out, and they sit in twilight now, or
> have vanished. The Jew saw them all beat them all, and is
> now what he always was, exhibiting no decadence, no
> infirmities of age, no weakening of parts, no slowing of his
> energies, no dulling of his alert and aggressive mind. All
> things are mortal but the Jew; all other forces pass, but
> he remains. What is the secret of his immortality?[12]

Though the modern State of Israel was reborn,
Jerusalem was not completely in their hands, and the
Temple Mount was still in the control of others. Between
1948 and 1967 the area of the Temple Mount was off limits
to Israelis. The liberation of the Old City would have to wait
another 19 years.

Endnotes

1. Steve Runciman, *A History of the Crusades,* Volume One, "The First Crusade," Cambridge University Press, 1951, p. 3.

2. Koran, Sura 17.

3. See our discussion in Chapter Ten.

4. Mishnah Berachot 9:5.

5. Cited by Solomon Steckoll, *The Temple Mount,* London. Tom Stacey Lt., 1972, p. 31.

6. Neil Asher Silberman, "In Search of Solomon's Lost Treasures," *Biblical Archaeological Review,* July/August, 1980, pp. 31-33.

7. Encyclopedia Judaica, Vol 4, p. 131.

8. Land grated to Israel was used to create a Palestinian state. Israel yielded the land for peace but the peace did not last.

9. Orde Wingate, cited by Michael Pragai, *Faith and Fulfillment,* London, p. 112.

10. *Time,* August 16, 1948.

11. The nation has returned but they are in unbelief. Confer Ezekiel 36:21-24.

12. Mark Twain, "Concerning the Jews," 1899.

CHAPTER SIX

JERUSALEM REGAINED: THE TEMPLE MOUNT STILL IN TURMOIL

By the rivers of Babylon, there we sat down, yea, we wept when we remembered Zion. We hung out harps upon the willows in the midst of it. For there those who carried us away captive required of us a song. And those who plundered us required of us mirth, saying, "Sing us one of the songs of Zion!" How shall we sing the Lord's song in a foreign land? If I forget you, O Jerusalem, let my right hand forget her skill! If I do not remember you, let my tongue cleave to the roof of my mouth—if I do not exalt Jerusalem above my chief joy (Psalm 137:1-6).

The city of Jerusalem is first mentioned about 1450 B.C. For all intents and purposes it should have fallen into oblivion. This city with no natural wealth, no oil reserves, and no great strategic value, is at the center of today's headlines. It is the focal point of debate among the great superpowers. No other city has been as desired and fought over as Jerusalem—the city of peace. In its history it has been fought by armies of the Babylonians, Persians, Greeks, Ptolemies, Seleucids, Romans, Byzantines, Arabs, Seljuks, Crusaders, Mongols, Mamelukes, Turks, British and Jordanians. Jerusalem has been a sacred symbol to three great religions: Judaism, Christianity and Islam.

All the eyes of the world are upon this city that has been sieged about forty different times and has been destroyed, at least partially, on thirty-two different occasions. The rule over Jerusalem has changed hands some twenty-six times. Since 1948 Jerusalem has experienced four wars.

Old City Liberated

In June 1967, the Jews were involved in a war that resulted in the liberation of the Old City of Jerusalem. On the third day of the Six Day War, Israeli Paratroop

Commander Motta Gur, mounted on a halftrack, announced that the Temple Mount had been regained.

On June 7 of that year, the Israeli troops moved into the Old City and stood at the Western Wall (Wailing Wall) for prayer. Rabbi Shlomo Goren declared:

> We have taken the city of God. We are entering the Messianic era for the Jewish people, and I promise . . . that what we are responsible for we will take care of.

The city of Jerusalem was reunified and the Star of David flew again from its ramparts.

Given Back to Moslems

On Saturday, June 17, 1967, shortly after the end of the Six Day War, Defense minister Moshe Dayan entered the Al Aqsa Mosque for a historic meeting. In an incredible gesture of good will, Dayan sat down on the prayer carpet with five leaders of the Supreme Moslem Council of formerly Jordan controlled Jerusalem. The subject was the Temple Mount and its administration. The discussion that day set Israel's policy regarding the Temple Mount. That policy remains in affect to this day.

Dayan had already ordered the Israeli flag removed from on top of the Dome of the Rock on the afternoon of the Old City's liberation. The discussion with the Moslems led to further concessions. The administrative control over the Temple Mount was to be the sole responsibility of the Supreme Moslem Council—the Waqf. Though the Jews would be permitted free access to the Mount, prayer or public worship by Jews was prohibited.

Dayan refused to permit any Jewish identification with Judaism's holiest site. To him, the Temple Mount held only historic interest. He said:

> I have no doubt that because the power is in our hands we must take a stand based on yielding. We must view the Temple Mount as a historic site relating to past memory.

The Israeli government then allocated responsibility of the Temple Mount area to different groups. Israel's Department of Antiquities was given the south, southeast and southwest area of the Temple Mount to excavate.

The top of the Temple Mount, however, the site of the First and Second Temple, was given to the Moslems to administrate. Though they allow tourists to visit they do not allow freedom of worship or any non-Moslem archaeological activity.

The Israeli citizens were largely apathetic about the Temple Mount ruling. Within the various religious factions there was no consensus of opinion about the holiness of the Temple Mount.

Defying the Order

Shortly after the Temple Mount was recaptured Rabbi Shlomo Goren the chief chaplain of the Israeli army, and one of the leading advocates for the rebuilding of the Temple, attempted to establish a Jewish identity with the Mount. The Western Wall below the Mount was all they possessed and to Goren that was not enough. He believed regaining the Mount would be a major step towards Israel's redemption.

On August 15, 1967, Goren led demonstrative Jewish prayers within the Temple Mount compound which was contrary to the newly agreed arrangement with the Israeli government. The Waqf responded by locking the entrance gate above the Western Wall that leads to the Temple Mount. The keys to that gate were confiscated soon thereafter and military police have been on duty at the entrance gate since that time. The public demonstration caused shock and apprehension among Moslems as to the fate of their sacred sites.

The chief Rabbis then compiled a statement forbidding Jews to visit the Temple Mount. They said the people were unclean and might accidently tread on the place where the Holy of Holies stood in the Temple.

The prohibition was then extended. The Rabbis said that there is not to be any exploration, excavation or even prayer on the Temple Mount.

Orthodox Jews and the Temple Mount

The thing that has done more to minimize tensions between Jews and Arabs concerning the Temple Mount is a ban on its entrance by the Chief Rabbinate of Israel. Though the ban does not carry any legal weight, it does keep some religious Jews from entering the Mount.

At the entrance to the Temple Mount the following sign is posted as a warning to Jews:

NOTICE AND WARNING

Entrance to the area of the Temple Mount is forbidden to
everyone by Jewish Law owing to the sacredness of the
place.

The Chief Rabbinate of Israel

Jews are banned from setting foot on the Temple
platform. The orthodox Jews generally observe the ban
while other Jews do not. The reason for the ban is that
Gentiles, as well as Jews, are regarded as "unclean" today
and are thus unfit to walk on the sacred Mount. The
Mount is considered so sacred that one is forbidden even
to fly over it because the holiness of the site extends into
the heavens. Therefore the orthodox Jew is allowed only to
admire the Mount from a distance. This ban will stay in
effect until the Messiah comes. Because of the ban, the
Jews worship at the Western Wall or "Wailing Wall" below
the Temple Mount.

When the Herodian Temple stood, stone plaques, some
in Latin, others in Greek, were placed warning any Gentile
not to enter the precincts of the Temple at the risk of
losing his life. A number of these signs were found reading:

No Gentile is to approach within the balustrade round
the Temple and the peribolos. Whosoever is caught will be
guilty of his own death which will follow.

While there were no such signs in later times when the
enclosure became a sacred place for Islam, Moslems were
no less jealous to guard the area from the steps of non-
Moslems. Threats to kill people trying to enter are
recorded in the reports of travellers who came to
Jerusalem in the past. The restrictions were partially lifted
in the middle of the nineteenth century but were clamped
down again when Arab nationalism rose to a peak under
the then Jerusalem Mufti, Haj Amin el Husseini, during
the thirties of the twentieth century.

The Waqf only permits limited access on the Temple
Mount. Sometimes for only a few hours a day and at other
times no access whatsoever. There is no religious activity
allowed on the Mount for Jews or Christians. Still the
Temple Mount is the center of Jerusalem:

The Temple Mount is the red-hot heart of the city. This
doesn't mean that everyone who lives here turns up there
in the course of a day, a week, a month or a year, or even
turns his mind to it. He may go through years without

giving it a thought, just as a Roman might not think of St. Peter's. Some young Jerusalemites, who can't remember a time when Jews couldn't freely and safely go to the Wall, do take it for granted. Yet even they know that Jerusalem, unlike Rome, is contested. They believe too that whoever holds the Holy Places, and especially the Temple Mount, possesses the upper hand in the city, and therefore the country.[1]

Political Issue

The current Supreme Moslem Council looks to a 1931 decision that the Temple Mount is exclusive Waqf property. The Waqf, who owes their allegiance to Jordan, does not accept the reunification of Jerusalem.

Prior to 1967, the central structure on the Mount for the Moslems was the Al Aqsa Mosque. After the city was recaptured in 1967, the Waqf began to term the entire Temple Mount as Al Aqsa. In effect, they annexed the entire Mount.

Ministry of Religious Affairs

The Ministry of Religious Affairs has not been sympathetic to those who wish freedom of worship on the Temple Mount. On June 27, 1967, the day the law regarding the Holy Places was adopted, the Minister of Religious Affairs said, "It is our standing afar and our disinclination to enter, that illustrate our awe and reverence over the site of our former Temples."

After the city of Jerusalem was reunified the Knesset (Israeli Parliament) passed a law which guaranteed freedom of access and worship in all the holy sites. This is enforced with one notable exception—the Temple Mount. Though freedom of worship is guaranteed, any open display of worship is not allowed. The carrying of a prayer book or the attempt to pray on the Mount is not allowed. The police believe that such an act is a threat to the peace because of Moslem reaction. Hence the Temple Mount is treated differently than all the rest of the holy sites in Israel.

On four different occasions the High Court of Justice has heard pleas from Jews to permit freedom of worship on the Temple Mount. Each time they have been denied.

One of the reasons that this has not caused more of a furor is a ban on the entrance to the Temple Compound that has been published by the Chief Rabbinate of Israel.

Limited Area

The former chief Rabbi Shlomo Goren believes that only a small part of the Temple Mount area, some 15 percent, is off limits to the people. Goren has attempted to measure the area to pinpoint where a worshipper can or cannot stand. It is his contention that worshippers should be allowed in the large area of the Temple Compound that does not constitute the sacred portions. The problem is that there is no consensus of opinion as to where to measure to indicate what parts are sacred and what parts are not.

PRESENT DAY GEOGRAPHY OF THE MOUNT

Today a visitor can enter the Old City of Jerusalem by one of seven gates. The present walls around the Old City were built from 1537 to 1541 by Sultan Suleiman the Magnificent after the Ottoman conquest of Israel. At that time most of the ancient walls were reduced to rubble. Suleiman ordered that Jerusalem be fortified to protect its people against marauding Bedouins.

The walls were rebuilt upon the foundations of the walls constructed during the time of the Second Temple and the later Roman expansion. For the most part, the modern gates of the city have little Biblical significance.

Eastern Gate

The outer gate of the sanctuary, which faces east toward the Mount of Olives, is the one known as the Golden Gate or Eastern Gate. In Arabic it is called *Bab ed Dahariyeh*, the Eternal Gate. It would have been the entrance to the city which Jesus used when He rode into Jerusalem on His triumphal entry. The present Golden Gate dates back to the Byzantine times (7th Century). It was built over the original Eastern Gate. The pillars of the gate are said to have been a gift from the Queen of Sheba to Solomon.

The Eastern Gate has been shut up since Jerusalem fell into Moslem hands. The only exception is when the Crusaders liberated the city A.D. 1102-1187. The Bible says that the Messiah will ride in through this East Gate.

Then he brought me back by the way of the outer gate of the sanctuary, which faces the east; and it was shut. And the Lord said to me. "This gate shall be shut; it shall not be opened and no one shall enter by it, for the Lord God of Israel has entered by it; therefore it shall be shut. As for the prince, He shall sit in it as prince to eat bread before the Lord; he shall enter by way of the porch of the gate, and shall go out by the same way" (Ezekiel 44:1-3).

In 1898 Kaiser Wilhelm was to enter the city through this gate in his ceremonial entry. However he chose to enter through the opposite side of the city.

When Jordan attempted to open it in 1967, they lost control of the city.

The Western Wall

The Western Wall is a quarter- mile long retaining wall that formed the western boundary of the Temple Mount. A 185 foot section that is exposed is an open air prayer area also known as the "Wailing Wall." The Western Wall was not part of the Temple. Rather it was one of the four retaining walls that surrounded the Temple Mount supporting the platform on which the Temple formerly stood. It was built by Herod the Great in order to enlarge the Temple Mount so that he could enlarge the worship area, beautify it and add more buildings to the Temple complex. When the Romans destroyed the Temple in A.D. 70 they left standing most of the retaining walls to commemorate the magnitude of their victory. It is the only remaining portion of the Second Temple.

Temple Mount

The Temple Mount, which rises above the Old City of Jerusalem is enormous. Archaeologist Meir Ben-Dov writes:

The dimensions of the Temple Mount in Jerusalem, the largest site of its kind in the ancient world, were as follows: the southern wall, the shortest of the retaining walls, is 280 meters long; the eastern wall is 460 meters; the western and longest wall of the retaining walls is 485 meters; and the northern wall is 315 meters. The Temple Mount is therefore a trapezoid covering 144,000 square meters. Twelve soccer fields—bleachers included—would fit into this area![2]

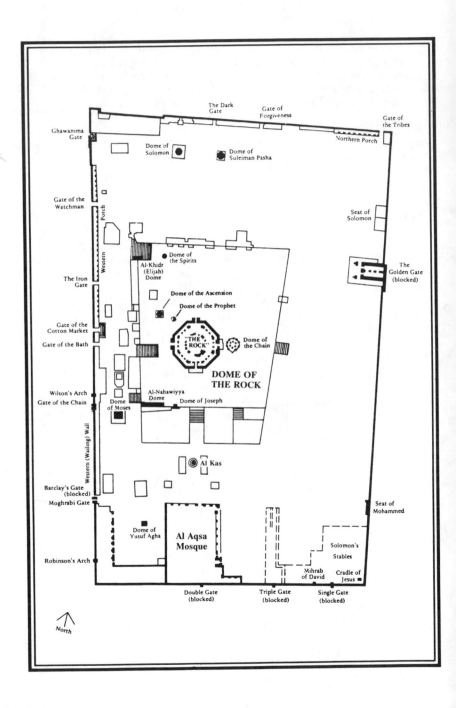

The Dark Gate

Gate of Forgiveness

Gate of the Tribes

Ghawanima Gate

Dome of Solomon

Dome of Suleiman Pasha

Northern Porch

Gate of the Watchman

Seat of Solomon

Western Porch

Dome of the Spirits

Al-Khidr (Elijah) Dome

The Iron Gate

Dome of the Ascension

Dome of the Prophet

The Golden Gate (blocked)

Gate of the Cotton Market

Gate of the Bath

"THE ROCK"

Dome of the Chain

DOME OF THE ROCK

Wilson's Arch

Gate of the Chain

Al-Nahawiyya Dome

Dome of Moses

Dome of Joseph

Western (Wailing) Wall

Al Kas

Barclay's Gate (blocked)

Moghrabi Gate

Seat of Mohammed

Dome of Yusuf Agha

Al Aqsa Mosque

Solomon's Stables

Robinson's Arch

Mihrab of David

Cradle of Jesus

Double Gate (blocked)

Triple Gate (blocked)

Single Gate (blocked)

North

The Temple Esplanade

On the Noble Sanctuary as the Moslems call it (Arabic *Haram esh-Sharif*) there are various structures including domes, prayer niches (mihrabs), fountains and arcades that decorate the area. In the course of time the Temple Mount acquired a large number of fountains and small shrines as gifts. In the compound today there are about 100 structures, both large and small.

As a person enters the Temple Mount from the Mograbi Gate there is an Islamic Museum immediately to their right. The Islamic Museum contains a good collection of Byzantine and Islamic antiquities. Slightly east of the Museum is the Al Aqsa Mosque, Islams third holiest site.

North of the Mosque is the Al Kas Fountain. It is used by the Moslems for ritual washing before prayer. Built in A.D. 709, it is attached to numerous underground cisterns.[3]

At the top of eight stairways are the Graceful Arcades which leads to the raised platform of the Mount. According to Moslem tradition, scales to weigh the souls of humanity will be hanged from these Arcades at the end of time.

The Dome of the Chain, constructed in the 8th Century, was used as a treasury by Arabs to store silver. When the Crusaders conquered the Mount they dedicated it as a chapel to St. James the Less. The structure has six inner and eleven outer supporting pillars. They can all be seen simultaneously when viewed from any angle. It is also called the "Tribunal of the prophet David." Arab legend says it was built by King David to pronounce judgment. It is believed that a large chain suspended from the Dome served as a lie-detector to those who were testifying. If a witness lied while holding onto the chain one of the links was said to have fallen out.

The most famous structure on the Mount is, of course, the famous Dome of the Rock. This shrine, built in the seventh century, is one of the most well-known buildings in the world. It houses the sacred rock that is thought by many to be the place where Abraham built the altar to sacrifice Isaac. It is also believed to be an essential part of the First and Second Temple.

The Dome of the Ascension, built around A.D. 1200, commemorates Mohammad's leap into the heavens. It is a copy of a Byzantine Dome on the Mount of Olives that marks the spot of Jesus' Ascension.

Solomon's Stables, at the southeast corner of the Temple Esplanade, was built by Herod to support the

Temple platform. They were possibly built on the remains of Solomon's Temple. This area was used by Herod and the Crusaders as stables.

Though Moslems consider the entire Mount to be sacred, when they pray facing Mecca they do it with their backs to the Dome of the Rock.

CONFRONTATIONS ON THE MOUNT

Since 1967, there have been various confrontations between Jews and Arabs on the Temple Mount.

On August 21, 1969, Michael Rohan a non-Jewish tourist from Australia set fire to the Al Aqsa Mosque. Firefighters fought the blaze for four hours as an angry Moslem crowd shouted "Down with Israel." The president of the Moslem Council accused the fire brigades of a deliberately slow response. The Arab states blamed Israel for the incident though Rohan identified himself as a "Church of God" member.

The fire destroyed a priceless wood and ivory pulpit (minbar) that had been sent from Aleppo by Saladin.

At his trial Rohan told the court that he believed himself to be "the Lord's emissary" in accordance with a prophecy in the Book of Zechariah. The court convicted Rohan but declared him criminally insane. He was placed in an Israeli mental hospital. The Temple Mount was closed to non-Moslems for two months after the incident. For the next three years, all non-Moslems were barred from the Al Aqsa Mosque.

After the ban was lifted the Moslem guards were still very nervous. The mere opening of a purse for a handkerchief would cause the guards to come running and search for a bomb.

Allen Harry Goodman

On April 11,1982, Allen Harry Goodman, an Israeli soldier, went on a shooting rampage on the Temple Mount. Storming into the Al Aqsa Mosque with an M-16 rifle Goodman killed a Moslem guard and wounded other Arabs. This incident set off a week of rioting and strikes in Jerusalem, the West Bank, and the Gaza Strip. At his trial Goodman told the court that he had expected to become "King of the Jews" by liberating this holy spot. He was convicted a year later and sentenced to life plus two terms of twenty years.

Yoel Lerner

In October 1982, Yoel Lerner, a member of Meir Kahane Kach movement, was arrested for planning to sabotage one of the sacred Moslem sites on the Temple Mount.

Lerner was convicted of planning to blow up the Dome of the Rock. Previously he had served a three year sentence for heading a group that plotted to overthrow the government and establish a state based upon religious law. He was sentenced to two and one half years in prison.

Foiled Raid on the Mount

On March 10, 1983 the police stopped an attempted raid on the Mount. Security forces arrested 45 Israelis foiling an armed raid on the Temple Mount to seize Moslem and Jewish holy places.

Israeli Security forces, working on a tip, captured ten men carrying army rifles, hoes and crowbars near an ancient passageway to the area in East Jerusalem.

Interior Minister Yosef Burg, the nation's internal security chief, assured leaders of the Supreme Moslem Council that authorities would stop any possible attacks of worshipers or attempts to curtail freedom of worship. Jerusalem Police Chief Yehoshua Caspi said a takeover "could have caused a most serious conflagration" between Arabs and Jews.

Twenty-nine people werc eventually charged for the intrusion but were acquitted of all charges.

Jerusalem Day 1983

On May 11, 1983 the Israeli high court of Justice ordered a very limited lifting of the ban of worship on the Temple Mount Compound. The court ordered the Jerusalem police to permit members of the "Faithful of the Temple Mount" to enter a small corner of the Temple precincts to worship for an hour and a half. The service commemorated Jerusalem Day, the anniversary of the reunification of the Holy City. Hundreds of worshippers crowded into the tiny area, defined by a rim of police barricades stretching but fifteen feet from the Mograbi Gate. The entire space allowed for Jewish worship was approximately seven hundred square feet, between 3:30 p.m. and 5:00 p.m., on Jerusalem Day.

The court order was controversial. Many Moslems saw it as an infringement of their religious sovereignty over the

Temple Mount. More secular Jews feared that the court's decision would simply complicate the already delicate relationships with the Arabs.

Many religious Jews celebrated the decision, declaring that Jerusalem cannot truly be considered liberated until a Jew has the right to share the Temple Mount with other religions in the worship of the Almighty.

Some of the Rabbis called for more severe restrictions to the point of allowing the Mount to be in permanent Moslem control so as to prevent Jews from entering it altogether.

Break in the Wall

In the summer of 1983, Rabbi Yehuda Getz broke through the Western Wall into a water cistern, hoping to eventually reach the foundation of the Second Temple. The Waqf discovered the underground activity and sent down some young men to discourage the work. A fist fight resulted and the episode concluded with the sealing of the wall with six feet of reinforced cement.

Lifta Band

On January 27, 1984, the most ambitious plan to assault the Temple Mount occurred. A group called the "Lifta Band," evidently wanting to hasten the coming of the Messiah, attempted to blow up the Moslem Holy sites on the Temple Mount.

Six to eight men, armed with at least 30 pounds of explosives and 22 Israeli army-issue hand grenades scaled the outer wall before dawn and slipped under the cover of a cloudy sky onto the compound that contains the mosques. They headed toward the Dome of the Rock.

An unarmed Moslem guard noticed them and alerted Israeli police, who chased them off. The intruders left behind explosives, ropes, ladders and knapsacks. Palestinian sources alleged that the amount of dynamite left was nearly 10 times what police have reported.

Media reports of aborted attack were censored for nearly two days. Israeli military censors prohibited publication of the news in Arabic-language newspapers published for some 36 hours.

Aftershocks

The attempted bombing of Islam's third-holiest sight created aftershocks in both the Jewish and Arab sectors of Jerusalem. The residents shuddered at the thought of what might have happened if the Dome of the Rock or the Al Aqsa Mosque had been destroyed by dynamite.

The Supreme Moslem Council, which supervises the shrine, warned, "If the attempted explosions had succeeded, all Arab countries would have immediately launched a holy war against Israel."

One dental technician in West Jerusalem said, "There would have been riots and mass murder. And you know, I wouldn't have blamed the Arabs. What would we do if Arab fanatics blew up the Western (Wailing) Wall?"

The attempted attack sparked isolated riots in Nablus and a nearby refugee camp on the so-called West Bank.[4] Arab commentators in the Middle East claimed that if the bombing had been successful, it would have started a new *jihad*, or holy war, against Israel.

Bishara Bahbah, the editor in chief of East Jerusalem's *Al-Fajr* newspaper, said, "It would have been the disaster of the decade,"

Anonymous callers claimed responsibility on behalf of a group calling itself Terror Against Terror.

Not the Last Attempt

After the foiled attempt on the Mount, the Jerusalem Temple Foundation issued the following statement:

The latest attempted assault on the Temple Mount will not be the last as long as the present injustice prevails. Police and soldiers and violence and barbed wire could be dispensed with, and peace reign if one simple basic condition were fullfilled—namely freedom of worship for all faiths on the Temple Mount as provided by Israeli law and as confirmed by the high court of Israel. The rule of Israeli law must be observed and upheld.[5]

Arrests and Convictions

Yehuda Cohen, one of the members of the assault group, was sentenced to one and one half years in prison for his part in the conspiracy. Cohen confessed to scouting the security arrangement of the Temple Mount as his part in blowing up the Dome of the Rock. He later expressed remorse over his actions. The judge, Ezra Hedaya, stressed the gravity of the crime.

> I won't exaggerate if I say that the aim of the conspiracy—to blow up the Dome of the Rock, holy to many millions of Moslems around the world is shocking, and constitutes a threat to public order and endangers the public. Who knows what would have been the consequences of the conspiracy.[6]

Sheikh Sa'ad Din Alami, the head of the Islamic Supreme Council for the Waqf and Islamic Holy places, reacted in the following manner to various journalists concerning Jewish attempts to regain the Temple Mount:

> The Temple Mount belongs to Moslems. Moslems only hate the Jew as a ruler. The Jews are free to believe that the Temple Mount is sacred to them, but I think that it is holy to me. To permit them a corner for prayer is against the Koran.

> There are no Jewish remains on the Mount. There never were Jewish antiquities here.

> They must know that this is a mosque and they cannot pray in a mosque with a Sefer Torah.[7]

From these responses it is clear that the Moslems officially disdain any attempts by the Jews to have a presence on the Mount.

Members of Parliament

Some members of the Israeli Parliament have accused the Arabs of stashing arms on the Temple Mount. The area of the South-eastern corner of the Mount is forbidden to all but the Moslem guard. This area, known as Solomon's stables, is reportedly an arms dump and there have been outcries from many Jews that the government investigate this and take action.

On January 8, 1986, a group of Knesset members including those who believe that the Jews have a right to pray upon the Temple Mount, gathered to investigate charges that arms were being stored beneath the Dome of the Rock and that archaeological sites were being destroyed. Because of the growing number of Jews who wish to rebuilt the Temple, it is believed that Moslems were systematically destroying any evidence of the previous Temples.

When the group of Knesset members reached Solomon's stables, there were informed that no cameras were allowed below the ground. Assuming the Moslems had something to hide the Israelis demanded that they take their cameras with them. The Moslem authorities (Waqf) confronted the delegation and a fight broke out. Atop a Moslem minaret, a loudspeaker announced that the Jews were attempting to commandeer the Temple Mount. A near riot occurred and the legislators decided to leave.

They returned six days later with one member reading aloud from Psalm 123 and others praying aloud. This caused another disturbance of the peace. They were never able to check for the hidden arms.

An Arab delegate in Morocco responded to this event by calling for Islamic countries to "wage a *jihad* (holy war) in all its forms until Jerusalem is liberated."

Flag Waving at Gate

Following the visit of the Knesset members to the Mount, three young people hoisted an Israeli flag over the Mograbi Gate of the Temple Mount. The flag was flying for about three minutes before they were arrested by police officers who removed the flag. The demonstrators were arrested for civil disturbance. The Sheik reacted to those events.

> I condemn these actions in the strongest possible terms and demand that the keys be returned to the Waqf immediately, that the police be reminded that the Mosque is an Islamic holy shrine, whose gates only Moslems are entitled to open or seal off, and that the army and border police be forbidden to enter the Mosque area. Thousands of years ago, the Jews built a temple which was subsequently destroyed. During the period of the second Caliph, Omar Ben Khatab, a mosque was built on the southern part of the yard of Al-Aqsa Mosque. At that time, there were neither temples for the Jews, nor churches for the Christians on the site and no building was destroyed. Historically, there is no proof that Al-Aqsa or the Dome of the Rock were built on the grounds of Solomon's Temple, although the Jews claim that the Temple originally stood on this site. The Moslems have been in charge of this piece of land for 14 centuries now and the Jews have no right to advocate the destruction of

our mosques because they want to rebuild Solomon's Temple.

It is impossible for any Jew to be allowed to pray in the grounds of the Al-Aqsa Mosque. They will have to kill all the Moslems before they can pray there unhindered.

Originally the Ottoman government designated a specific place from which police could ensure the security of the Mosque. The British and later the Jordanians and the Israelis used the same place as a police center. Then, the Israeli police were joined by border police. Following our protests, it was decided that the border police should merely man the doors of the Mosque area and would not actually wander in the grounds themselves, but this decision has subsequently been ignored, unfortunately.

The Islamic Council asked the Waqf to form a guard unit to protect the Mosque area day and night and survey all those entering. These guards have the authority to prohibit any non-Moslem from praying in the Mosque, and if necessary to use force in order to ensure that these rules are adhered to.[8]

Laying a Cornerstone?

On October 8, 1990, when the crisis in the Persian Gulf between the Allied Forces and Iraq was heating up, an incident took place on the Temple Mount that caught the attention of the world. The Temple Mount Faithful marched on the Mount and unfurled a banner denouncing the Moslem presence. News reports erroneously said that there were Jews attempting to lay a foundation stone for the Third Temple on the Temple Mount.

In the wake of the riot 22 Palestinians were killed. The United Nations censured Israel for overreacting to the incident. The United States, wishing to keep together the fragile coalition with Arab states against Iraq, voted against Israel. There was no censure of the Palestinians who started the riot.

Newsweek reported on the bloody clash that left over twenty Palestinians dead:

Last weeks clash was only the most bloody of several incidents in recent years in which young Arabs, rocks in hand, have rushed to ward off Jewish "attack." Their religious leaders teach that those who die defending the Noble Sanctuary go immediately to heaven. "If we give up one centimeter, if we let them place even one toe [on the mount] it will be the end of our holy places," said Muhammad Watani, a resident of the Old City. "It will be easier for us to die first." To Muslims, the deaths last week only deepened the sanctity of a place both faiths have long associated with glorious redemption and epic destruction.[9]

Newsweek also said it was . . .

a cycle of misunderstanding: following rumors of a Jewish "invasion," Palestinian youth rushed Israeli police on Al Aqsa plaza. When the police killed an Arab, the Palestinians replied with rocks, scattering worshipers at the Western Wall below. Enraged Israeli's fought back with live ammunition killing 21.[10]

What Really Happened?

This is what was commonly reported. But is that what really occurred? Mortimer Zuckerman, Editor-in-Chief of *U.S. News and World Report*, tells a different story:

The impression given to the world is that the Palestinians assembled at the Al Aqsa Mosque in order to confront a small band of Jewish Zealots, the Temple Mount Faithful, who have been intent on establishing a third Jewish temple on the Temple Mount. It is true the group planned a march—marches in previous years have been non-violent—but there was no march of the Faithful on the fateful Sunday. The Supreme Court of Israel had banned the demonstration. The Muslim Council, Wakf, a kind of mini—Vatican organization that the Israelis permit to rule the Muslim holy places on the Temple Mount, was informed of the Supreme Court ruling. All the Arab language newspapers in Jerusalem had published news stories about the Court's ban several days earlier, at the request of Israeli authorities. These efforts to keep the peace were frustrated because on the night before this holy day of Judaism, Palestinian-Arab activists recruited thousands of Arabs to come to this holy place where some 20,000 Jewish pilgrims—not the faithful zealots— would be praying on the adjacent plaza some 40 feet below the Western Wall.

Present on that day, in the mosque, was Faisal Husseini, a key Palestine Liberation Organization intifada leader, who is normally not seen at the mosque on a day that is not a special day of prayer for the Muslims. But not present on that day were the Wakf security personnel who had been surreptitiously withdrawn from the area between the gates, at the Western edge of the Mount that overlooked the Western Wall and the Jewish pilgrims gathering before it. Forty feet above them, the Arab youths assembled and did what they had been gathered to do. They rioted.[11]

Summary

Even though the Temple Mount has been regained, it is still being profaned. When the Mount fell into Jewish hands after the Six Day War, Israel took the Western Wall area but left administration of the Mount to the Moslem Council of Elders. Israel also banned Jewish worship. Efforts by a small number of Jews to pray on the Temple Mount have been frustrated by the police, the Moslem Waqf and the government in spite of the constitutional guarantees. Because the government of Israel is basically secular, Jewish pressure for prayer on the Temple Mount come from a minority of Israeli citizens. The issue is a stalemate.

Endnotes

1. Ed Grossman, Symbol and Madness, The Jerusalem *Post,* Local Supplement, September 30, 1983.

2. Meir Ben-Dov, *In the Shadow of the Temple,* Harper and Row Publishers, New York, 1982, p. 77.

3. This fountain could have been placed over the site of the Holy of Holies of the First and Second Temple. See Chapter Ten.

4. The term "West Bank" was coined by Israel's enemies. It refers to the Biblical land of Judea and Samaria.

5. Directive from Stanley Goldfoot of the *Jerusalem Temple Foundation.*

6. Jerusalem *Post,* International Edition, July 22-28, 1984, p. 8.

7. These references are found in the Middle Eastern Periodicals: *Koteret Rashit, Ha'aretz,* and *Hadashot.*

8. From the *Al Awdah* Weekly.

9. *Newsweek,* October 22, 1990.

10. *Newsweek,* ibid. p. 37.

11. Mortimer Zuckerman, *U.S. News and World Report,* November 12, 1990, pp. 95-96.

CHAPTER SEVEN

CURRENT PREPARATIONS TO BUILD A NEW TEMPLE

TO ALL PERSONS OF THE JEWISH FAITH ALL OVER THE WORLD—

A project to rebuild the Temple of God in Israel is now being started. With Divine Guidance and Help the "Temple" will be completed. Jews will be inspired to conduct themselves in such a moral way that our Maker will see fit to pay us a visit here on earth. Imagine the warm feeling that will be ours when this happy event takes place. "THIS IS MY GOD" is the book that was the inspiration for this undertaking. God will place in the minds of many persons in all walks of Jewish life the desire to participate in this work. Executive talent, Administrators, and Workers on all levels are needed. All efforts will be anonymous. GOD will know those desiring to participate.

Please write to Box M-917, *The Washington Post.* Under no circumstances send contributions.

"GOD'S WILL WILL PREVAIL"

The Ad, in one inch high letters, was placed in the *Washington Post,* on May 21, 1967 *before* Jerusalem was liberated.

From the time of the destruction of the Second Temple, there has been no real center for the Jews. They have not been able to perform their religious duties as the Scriptures call for. The synagogues are not the same thing as the Temple. They are places of prayer, reading, and training. The priesthood has been inactive since Jerusalem's fall. This was predicted in Scripture:

For the children of Israel will abide many days without a king and without a prince, and without a sacrifice, and without an image, and without an ephod and without teraphim (Hosea 3:4).

Pagan Structures

Although the entire city of Jerusalem is now under Israeli control, the Temple Mount is still in the hands of the Moslems. The Dome of the Rock and the Al Aqsa Mosque stand high upon the Mount providing a constant reminder that "pagan" holy places are on the site where their sacred Temple stood. The words of the prophet Ezekiel are as true today as ever:

> And their Holy Places shall be defiled . . . "Because the enemy has said. of you, 'Aha! even the ancient heights have become our possession' " (Ezekiel 7:24;36:2).

The current situation provides increasing incentive for the Jews to build a Third Temple.

Third Temple Preparations

Although the ban on visiting the Temple Mount remains in effect for Orthodox Jews, it has not stopped those in Israel from thinking about the realization of a long lost dream, the rebuilding of the Temple. Once the city of Jerusalem was retaken this was no longer a pipe dream. *Time* magazine reports:

> Since the destruction of Jerusalem by the Romans in A.D. 70, Conservative and Orthodox Jews have beseeched God four times a week to 'renew our days' as they once were—a plea for the restoration of the Temple. Although Zionism was largely a secular movement, one of its sources was the prayers of the Jews for a return to Palestine so that they could build a temple . . . Learned Jewish opinion has long debated when and how the temple can be rebuilt. The great medieval philosopher Maimonides, in his Code of Jewish Law, argued that every generation of Jews was obliged to rebuild the temple if its site was ever retaken, if a leader descended from David could be found, and if the enemies of Jerusalem were destroyed.[1]

Why Rebuild?

Number 20 of the 613 commandments in the Torah (according to ancient Jewish sage Maimonides) calls for the building of a Temple in Jerusalem if one does not exist or orders the maintainence of a Temple if it does exist.

Orthodox Jews during their exile called for the eventual building of the Temple in Jerusalem.

The question arises as to the incentives the Jewish people would have for constructing a new Temple. Why would they want to rebuild it? Two reasons come to mind. (1) The fulfillment of a dream. (2) A rallying point for the nation.

The first incentive would be the fulfillment of a dream. For centuries the Jews did not possess their homeland and were forced to wander as strangers and vagabonds across the face of the earth. Deep within their hearts has been a longing for the return to the land and a rebuilding of the Temple, for the Temple is also a symbol of prosperity and a reminder of better days that the nation had. The desire for the restoration of the Temple has been the prayer of the Orthodox Jew since the destruction of the Second Temple in A.D. 70.

A rebuilt Temple could also be a unifying force for this small beleaguered nation. During their relatively new existence as a reborn nation Israel has experienced a series of major wars. A house of worship could serve as a rallying point for Jews worldwide. Furthermore it could help unify the many Jewish factions that exist in Israel today.

The Jerusalem Post reports:

> The modern Jew found it difficult to face the binding obligation to rebuild the sanctuary, combined with the great dreams linked with it. He has suppressed the demands they make on him.
>
> He was hesitant to use religious language to describe the historic return to Zion and to national sovereignty. There are indeed a few exceptions to this, as for example, 'the Third Temple,' once used by Ben-Gurion or the excessive use of prophetic terminology of the 'ingathering of the exiles' during the years of mass aliya.
>
> Far beyond the formal commandment, the yearning to behold an actual concrete expression of a central religious and national focal point permeates all Jewish history.
>
> Another argument is that the rebuilding as postulated by Maimonides requires a certain order of events: 1) coming to the land; 2) appointment of a king from the house of David; 3) blotting out the descendants of Amalek; and only then 4) the building of the Temple. The counter argument claims that, while this is indeed the ideal order of events, the events themselves are not necessary mutually interdependent and one must carry out whichever is possible at the time.[2]

A United Front

In 1982, after years of squabbling, three groups of devout Jews, *The Jerusalem Temple Foundation*, *To the Mountain of the Lord* and *The Faithful of the Temple Mount* combined their forces to plan for and build the Third Temple. The following is an extract from their constitution.

PURPOSES:

a)   To undertake research into the history of Holy Places in Israel.

b)   To provide scientific means and equipment for the efficient investigation of such places and of archaeological sites.

c)   To study the religious, political, economic, social, cultural and ethnic aspects and implications of these investigations and explorations.

d)   To advance the learning and application of the scriptures.

e)   To work for the safeguarding and preservation of the integrity of Holy Places in Israel, and their restoration, with special emphasis on the Temple Mount.

f)   To provide a forum for authoritative discussion of matters falling with the Foundation's scope of interest.

g)   To publish the results and records of its discussions and research in order to endow the public with a wider knowledge of Holy Places and archaeological sites in Israel.

h)   To launch world-wide competitions for the design and construction of suitable edifices and similar projects in Israel.

i)   To raise funds for the promotion and development of these and allied activities.

Some of the Temple Mount activists view the matter in more nationalistic than religious terms. They see the Temple Mount as part of Israel and until the Mount is in Israeli control then Israel does not have complete sovereignty over its country.

One of their poets, Uri Zvi Greenberg, wrote, "Israel without the Mount—is not Israel. He who controls the Mount, controls the land of Israel."

Prayer

The Faithful of the Temple Mount have provided a prayer which they feel that all true believers in the God of Israel can pray.

A Prayer of the Nations from
THE FAITHFUL of the TEMPLE MOUNT JERUSALEM

Our Father which art in Heaven! Guard the children of all nations who perform Thy will and fear Thy great name. Bestow upon them Thy blessings for prosperity and brotherhood and peace. Instill in the hearts of all the faith that Thou art alone G-d[3] in heaven above and on the earth below.

Let all men call on Thy name and serve Thee with undivided heart. Bring near that day on which a multitude of nations will go forth and say, "Come, let us go to the Mount of the Lord, to the House of the G-d of Jacob, and He will teach us of His ways, and we will walk in His paths-for out of Zion shall go forth the Law, and the word of the Lord from Jerusalem."

Save thy people Israel in the Holy Land, and grant her sons the strength to withstand the foes who rise against them. Open the eyes and hearts of their neighbors that they should know that only in Israel's peace will they enjoy peace. Let them understand that the Word of G-d came to the forefathers of this nation to grant them this Land-as it is written in the Law of Moses, and as was promised throughout the prophets-that He will gather them from their dispersion, settle them on their soil, renew their Sanctuary, and reestablish their Kingdom as of old.

Awaken the hearts of the Children of Israel for whom You descended upon Mount Sinai to give them the Law and its commandments by the hand of Moses-to observe all that is written in Thy Law, in order that they should succeed in all they do, and thus to hasten the coming of their salvation, and the salvation of the world. AMEN.

Time For a New Temple?

On October 16, 1989, *Time* magazine ran an article titled, "Time For a New Temple?"

Next week Israel's Ministry of Religious Affairs will sponsor a first-ever Conference of Temple Research to discuss whether contemporary Jews are obligated to rebuild the Temple. However, several small organizations in Jerusalem believe the question is settled. They are zealously making preparation for the new Temple in spite of the doctrinal obstacles and the certainty of promoting Muslem fury.

Two Talmudic schools located near the Western Wall are teaching nearly two hundred students the elaborate details of Temple service. Other groups are researching the family lines of Jewish priests who alone may conduct sacrifices. Former Chief Rabbi Shlomo Goren, who heads another Temple Mount organization, believes his research has fixed location on the ancient Holy of Holies so that Jews can enter the Mount without sacrilege.

One difficulty is the requirement that priests purify their bodies with the cremated ashes of an unblemished red heifer before they enter the Temple. Following a go-ahead from the Chief Rabbinate, institute operatives spent two weeks in August scouting Europe for heifer embryos that will shortly be implanted into cows at an Israeli cattle ranch.

. . . historian David Solomon insists that a new Temple is essential: 'It was the essence of our Jewish being, the unifying force of our people . . . but sooner or later, in a week or a century, it will be done.

And we will be ready for it.' He adds with quiet urgency, 'Every day's delay is a stain on the nation.'4

Build a Synagogue

There has been more recent urges to build upon the Temple Mount. Some have launched the idea of building a synagogue. Though far short of the final goal of building a Temple, a synagogue would establish Jewish presence on the Mount for the first time in nineteen hundred years.

In August 1986, leading Israeli rabbis, including the former Ashkenazic Chief Rabbi Shlomo Goren, ruled that Jews are obligated to pray at a sanctuary to be built upon the Mount. Rabbi Goren believed that a 1967 survey of the Temple Mount showed the exact location of the First and Second Temples as well as the site of the Ark of the Covenant. Goren then determined the exact areas on the Temple Mount where a Jewish sanctuary could be constructed without violation of the ancient decree not to tread on holy soil. Thus a worshipper could pray at the Synagogue without treading upon "holy ground."

The ruling touched off a storm of controversy in Moslem circles. Goren said that the synagogue would not interfere with Moslem areas of the Mount.

Jews and Moslems already conduct prayers side by side at the Cave of Machpeleh in Hebron, site of the tombs of the Patriarchs.

Chief Rabbi Mordechai Eliahu has suggested that if a synagogue is built, it should be done on the Eastern Wall of the Temple Mount. Such a synagogue stood there until the 16th century. The entrance to the synagogue could be from outside the wall preventing people from walking upon the prohibited areas of the Mount.

This proposed synagogue has not yet been built and may never be built. It is, however, another attempt by the Jews to establish a presence upon the Temple Mount.

Preparations For a Third Temple

The ultimate dream is not a synagogue on the Temple Mount but rather a Third Temple. Preparations are already underway for its construction. The following ad was found in an English speaking newspaper in Jerusalem in April 1991.

One of the most active groups in Israel today is Atara Le Yoshna.   The goal of this group is to restore Jewish presence in the Old City of Jerusalem near the Temple Mount. This area is today the Moslem quarter. A brochure that they produce states the following:

> The Atara Le Yoshna was created by a group of concerned citizens . . . Its goal is to return the property of Old Jerusalem   to its rightful Jewish ownership-not by force or harassment, but through purchase or legal proceedings.

The Atara Le Yoshna had established a tourist and study center in the Old City. Scale models of the Tabernacle, the Temple, Ark of the Covenant, the Temple Vessels, Noah's Ark, as well as many others can be found in the study center.

They have done a clever thing with the scale model of the Ark of the Covenant. When a person stands in front of the model, he can see the actual Dome of the Rock through an open window. It is lined up directly with the scale model of the Temple. Since they believe their former Temples actually stood at the Dome of the Rock site, the model serves as a reminder of their former glory and the site on which they stood.

In addition, there is a large scale model of the Third Temple that is to be built in Jerusalem. It is modeled after the dimensions found in the Book of Ezekiel.[5]

One of the groups associated with Atara Le Yoshna is the yeshiva (school) Ateret Cohanim. The goal of this yeshiva is to prepare for the coming priesthood.

A New Priesthood

If a new Temple is to be constructed then there must be a functioning priesthood to perform the proper rites and ceremonies. Such a priesthood is now in the works. In an old stone building in the Old City of Jerusalem, a small group of young scholars are preparing for the building of the Third Temple and the coming of the Messiah.

The founder of Ateret Cohanim is Motti Hacohen. Hacohen had been challenged by a friend to become more interested in the Temple regulations seeing that he was from the priestly line. Hacohen decided to take up the challenge.

Hacohen then began a search for a yeshiva that could teach him matters concerning the rebuilding of the

Temple. Finding none that would satisfy his needs Hacohen founded the Ateret Cohanim.

The Yeshiva conducts seminars, a field school, and an annual convention on the subject of the Temple Mount. They also explore specific subjects such as animal sacrifices.

On Good Friday, 1990, one hundred and fifty Messianic Jews, members of the Ateret Cohanim, moved into four buildings in the Christian quarter of Jerusalem causing a protest from both Moslem and Christian groups. The site of the building, just around the corner from the church of the Holy Sepulchre, was chosen to help create Jewish settlements in the Old City of Jerusalem geographically near the Temple Mount.

Materials Ready

For years there have been rumors that precut stones have been cut in America and shipped to Israel for the building of the Third Temple. Evangelist John Wesley White wrote:

> Late in 1979 I was riding in Indiana with a local Presbyterian minister. At a certain point along the highway he informed me that we were driving past the gate of a company which purportedly handled a highly classified order of the finest building stones in the world. Sixty thousand tons of pre-cut stones had been shipped on 500 rail cars. They were allegedly bought by the Israeli Government, and had already arrived in Israel.[6]

This is highly unlikely. Anyone who has ever visited Israel will immediately be impressed that stones are everywhere. In fact, Israel actually exports them! Whether precut stones have already been made in Israel is another matter. Though rumors abound, no clear evidence has come forward to support this idea.

The Temple Institute

One group that is making implements is the Temple Institute. The Temple Institute makes no secret of the fact that they hope to see the soon rebuilding of the Temple. The Temple Institute was founded to fulfill the biblical command to "build a Temple" insofar as it is now possible. The Institute points out that about one third of the 613 commandments according to Jewish sage Maimomides are dependent upon an actual Temple existing in Jerusalem. The Temple Institute has spent years researching the materials, measurements and the forms of the 93 sacred vessels that are used in the Temple. They have begun construction of these vessels as well as the Priestly garments.[7] These vessels are not mere items for display. Though they now serve as educational tools it is the goal of the Temple Institute to use them when a Third Temple has been built. *Time* magazine reported:

> No group is more zealous than the Temple Institute, whose spiritual leader, fifty-year-old Rabbi Israel Ariel, was one of the first Israeli paratroopers to reach the Mount in 1967. 'Our task,' states the institute's American-born director, Zev Golan, 'is to advance the cause of the Temple and prepare for its establishment, not just talk about it.'[8]

The group is preparing for the Third Temple. In a brochure they have produced, the Temple Institute states its aims:

> The dream of the Temple is as old as the Jewish people itself. Even on the Red Sea, only minutes after G-d's miraculous salvation of Israel, Moses raises his voice in song: "You will bring them and plant them on the mountain of your inheritance, the place where you have set for your dwelling, O L-rd, the Temple of God which your hands have established. . . "
>
> The hope for the rebuilding of the Temple was born on the very day of its destruction almost 2,000 years ago. Rabbi Akiva comforted his weeping colleagues by proclaiming that if the prophecies of destruction have come to pass, the fulfillment of the prophecy of redemption and rebuilding is certainly to follow. In the course of 2,000 years, the Jewish people have never forgotten the Temple. On our holidays we pray: "Build your house as at the first, set your Temple on its foundations, allow us to see it built and make us joyous in its establishment, return Priests to their service and Levites to their songs and music, and return Israel to their pleasant places, and there we will ascent and be seen and bow down before you . ." On our days of mourning we cry: "It would be a delight to my soul to walk naked and barefoot upon the desolate ruins of your Holy courts, in place of your Ark which has been hidden . . ." At our most joyous we break a glass to remember its destruction.
>
> The dream of rebuilding the temple spans 50 generations of Jews, five continents and innumerable

seas and oceans. The prayer for the rebuilding is recited in as many languages as are known to humanity. These prayers are recited in prisons and ghettos, study halls and synagogues, homes and fields everyday for 2,000 years of exile, in the face of poverty and persecution and seemingly hopeless peril, now gain a new dimension with the return of the people of Israel to the Land of Israel, with the rebirth of the Jewish state and the creation of a Jewish army and the flowering of the desert and the scientific and social strides made by the nation of Israel. This new dimension is: a Possibility.

The Temple Institute receives visitors and conducts tours. In the exhibition hall some of the implements for the Third Temple are on display.

The Institute is a blend of the old and the new. To research these ancient implements modern technology is used including the most advanced computer programs.

The Royal Purple and the Biblical Blue

Attention to the most minute detail is what characterizes the individuals who are attempting to prepare for a new Temple and a new priesthood. One problem that is yet to be solved concerns two colors used in the Temple garments. They are the royal purple (argaman in Hebrew) and the Biblical (or ritual) blue (tekhelet in Hebrew). They were two of the most important colors in the culture of ancient Israel, as well as that of non-Jewish nations. These two dyes were made from marine snails and were important not only for the economy of ancient maritime civilizations but also had social, religious and even political implications as well. There are intense studies by experts from all over the world to ascertain the precise nature of the dye industry of ancient Israel and to locate the particular species of snail which yielded these particular ritual colors.

Talmudic sources state[9] that the tekhelet sea-snail comes up from the sea once in seventy (or seven) years. Such extreme rarity is apparently not to be taken literally, despite recent colorful, but fanciful, stories about the snails.[10]

The search for these exact colors still goes on. This thorough research is typical of the commitment that is held with regard to the Temple and its implements.

Gershon Salomon and the Temple Mount Faithful

One of the major figures of the Temple Mount movement is Gershon Salomon, head of the Temple Mount Faithful. For the last few years, the Temple Mount Faithful has attempted to lay a cornerstone for the Third Temple on Jerusalem Day. Each time they have been stopped by the authorities. In a 1991 interview with the Jerusalem *Post*, Salomon made the following relevant statements concerning his efforts to build a Third Temple:

JP: Your announcement last October that you would lay the cornerstone for the Third Temple reportedly set off a chain of events that led to the Temple Mount riot, and killing of Jews in reprisal. Do you feel guilty?

Salomon: Not at all. The Palestinians and Saddam Hussein decided to refocus the attention of the world on Israel. They wanted to use us as an excuse. The fact is that we were prevented from going up to the Temple Mount. If they hadn't fomented trouble there, they would have elsewhere.

JP: Do you have a personal message from God?

Salomon: Everyone predicted I would die from my war wounds. In hospital, I realized the spirit is much stronger than the body. There is no reason for me to live unless I have a mission.

JP: If you had a free hand to accomplish that mission, what would you do?

Salomon: I would remove the Moslem presence from the Temple Mount, announce to the world that the Temple Mount is the center for the Jewish people, and start building a Third Temple. . .

JP: Would you destroy the Dome of the Rock and the al-Aqsa Mosque?

Salomon: No I'd move them. Maybe to Mecca.

JP: Both structures have been standing where they are since the seventh century. Don't they have some right to remain there?

Salomon: Islam's conquests were entirely imperialistic. Everywhere the Moslem's went Jewish and Christian places were transformed into mosques. The night after my guard duty on the Temple Mount, in the Six Day War, an old Arab showed me around, and pointed to the place where the Temple had stood. He was sure we'd start ground breaking immediately.

JP: How do you view the reversion of the Temple Mount to Moslem authority in 1967?

Salomon: A national tragedy. The event should be mourned.

JP: Why did then-defense minister Moshe Dayan do it?

Salomon: I can only think that the Israeli leadership was not ready for that historic moment.

JP: Are they ready now?

Salomon: I think so. We're at the 11th hour.

JP: Leaflet 65, published by the leadership of the Intifada, included a list of Jews on whom the death sentence has been passed. You were Number One. How do you explain that high ranking?

Salomon: The Arabs understand, better than the Jews, that the battle over the Temple Mount and Jerusalem is central. They view me as more the enemy of Islam than generals and politicians. . .

JP: How many supporters do you have?

Salomon: We have 9,000 on our membership list and I'm always receiving phone calls from Jews and Christians abroad. they urge me to push ahead with this work. I can't walk down the street without people shaking my hand and wishing me strength to continue. I can't believe there are many Jews who don't dream of having a Third Temple. . . I believe you have to work actively as an agent of God for the Redemption to occur. I totally reject the approach of Jews waiting passively for the Messiah.

JP: You are an observant Jew, yet you don't observe the Rabbinical ruling not to tread on the Temple Mount. Why is that?

Salomon: Most rabbi's do not accept this ruling, which reflects Diaspora thinking. It is a ruling which has run contrary to Jewish interests. In the same way, all the attention given to the Kotel [the Western Wall]- which is merely an exterior wall of the Temple-is Diaspora thinking. I would close down the prayer area at the Kotel and make it into a museum . . . rabbis agree with me. Rabbi Goren, for instance. And the Sephardic Chief Rabbi Mordehai Eliahu wants to open a study room on the Temple Mount. . .

JP: Do you have an actual cornerstone ready?

Salomon: Yes, a four-ton marble stone hewed at Mitzpe Rimon without metal tools. It's near the Old City now.

JP: Did you wear a gas mask during the missile attacks?

Salomon: No. No one can hurt me in Jerusalem. Following a stunning Allied victory, Israel will be admired as never before. I assume that soon we will receive permission to start rebuilding the Temple. No force can stop the process of building the Land of Israel. We are approaching a climax. The Arab conquest of Jerusalem will be done with once and for all. All the important government buildings will be moved to the Old City, and the voice of Israel will emanate from there.[11]

Like all of the other groups, Salomon and the Temple Mount Faithful are committed to see a Third Temple built in Jerusalem in the near future.[12]

Ark of the Covenant

One of the important issues surrounding a Third Temple concerns the long lost Ark of the Covenant. What will be its place, if any, in the Third Temple?

The last biblical mention of the Ark is 2 Chronicles 35:3 where it is placed back into the Temple in the realm of King Josiah. After that there is silence. There was no Ark in the Second Temple.

There is no concrete evidence today that the Ark still exists or that someone has it, though there are many theories as to its possible location. Though the discovery of the Ark of the Covenant is not essential to the building of the Third Temple, if it were found the Ark would provide incalculable momentum to construct a new Temple.

Ashes of the Red Heifer

Some insist that one of the requirements necessary for a Third Temple is the sacrifice of the ashes of the red heifer. The ashes of the red heifer were used to purify the people from defilement.

> Now the Lord spoke to Moses and Aaron saying . . . 'Speak to the children of Israel, that they bring you a red heifer without blemish, in which there is no defect and on which never a yoke has come. You shall give it to Eleazar the priest, that he may take it outside the camp, and it be slaughtered before him; and Eleazar the priest shall take some of its blood on his finger, and sprinkle some of its blood seven times directly in front of the tabernacle of meeting' (Numbers 19:1-4).

After this was done the priest would take the ashes of the burned red heifer and store them in a place outside of the camp of Israel.

When the First Temple was built in Jerusalem, the priest sacrificed the red heifer from the Mount of Olives. Each time a sacrifice was performed the ashes were mixed with the previous ones to provide an unbroken chain to the original red heifer.

There is an account in one of the Dead Sea Scrolls (the Copper Scroll) that a red heifer was sacrificed prior to the destruction of Jerusalem in A.D. 70. The ashes were said to have been taken from the Temple before its destruction and secretly buried.

The search for the original ashes of the Red Heifer is being carried on today in Israel. If the original ashes are not found there are plans to sacrifice a new red heifer— if an appropriate candidate can be found. There are however, others who insist that this ritual is not necessary for the purification of the Temple.

The Third Temple and the Coming Messiah

Today there are many Jews who expect the Messiah to be the one who builds the Third Temple. They are not concerned with the preparations for a new Temple because they do not believe it is their responsibility. Consequently they do not get involved in issues such as freedom of worship on the Temple Mount or any of the other matters that the aforementioned groups have dedicated themselves.

The rabbinical view is the Messiah is not the divine "Son of God" as Christians believe. He will be a man, not God. He will be a combination of an Elijah, Solomon and David.

While Christians believe the Messiah has already come, Judaism is waiting for His arrival. One Jewish leader said:

They believe that once the Temple is built, Jesus will come again. We expect the Messiah to come for the first time. Let's build the Temple, and see what he looks like.[13]

Summary

Today the Temple Mount remains in turmoil. As certain groups are preparing to build a Third Temple, government forces in Israel as well as the Moslem powers that be, are keeping this from occurring. The secular Jews do not care and many of the Orthodox Jews believe that the Third Temple will have to await the arrival of the Messiah.

The Temple will be built—the Bible says so. The Jews will receive a Messiah but will He be the real one?

Endnotes

1. "Should the Temple be Rebuilt," *Time,*   June 30, 1967.

2. Pinchas H. Pell, "A Place for the Lord," Jerusalem *Post,* February 11, 1989.

3. The Divine Name is not spelled out due to reverence.

4. "Time for a New Temple?" *Time,* October 16, 1989.

5. See a suggested model of Ezekiel's Temple in Appendix 5.

6. John Wesley White, *The Coming World Dictator,* Minneapolis, Bethany Fellowship, 1981, p. 90.

7. See our pictures in the photo section.

8. *Time* ibid.

9. Talmudic Encyclopedia, (Jerusalem) 15, 530-534 (in Hebrew) 1976.

10. *The Royal Purple and the Biblical Blue, Argaman and Tekhelet,.* The study of Chief Rabbi Dr. Isaac Herzog on the Dye Industries in Ancient Israel and Recent Scientific Contributions, Keter Publishing House, Jerusalem Ltd. p. 212.

11. Jerusalem *Post,* International Edition, Week Ending April 13, 1991.

12. The groups we have mentioned are not the only ones involved in the work to rebuild the Temple. They are merely some of the most visible.

13. Cited by Barbara and Michael Ledeen, The Temple Mount Plot, The New Republic, June 18, 1984, p. 23.

CHAPTER EIGHT

A "CHRISTIAN" CONNECTION

Some evangelical Christians have entered into the fight over the Temple Mount on behalf of the Jews. The Jerusalem Temple Foundation, for example, formed a branch in America. Those involved were evangelical Christians who, for various motives, want to help the Jews gain access to the Temple Mount and build a Third Temple. This group has lobbied extensively on behalf of the various Temple Mount groups. They have gone so far as to take out a one page ad in the Jerusalem *Post* condemning the Israeli government for arresting Temple Mount activists. (see p. 122).

Though well-intentioned, we believe some of these groups have gone too far in their desire to see a Third Temple built.[1]

The Media's Response

The press has taken an interest in the link between evangelical Christians and those in Israel who are associated with making the Temple Mount a free forum for worship.

In the magazine, *The New Republic*, an article appeared entitled "The Temple Mount Plot" by Barbara and Michael Ledeen. Over the title of the article the headline read, "What do Christian and Jewish fundamentalists have in common?" The article began as follows:

A casual observer might be excused for believing that nearly all of the recent violence in Israel has been part of the usual cycle of Arab-Israeli conflict. The observer would be wrong. Though some of the recent acts, such as the plans to place time bombs on Arab buses in Jerusalem, seem to be the work of extremist Israeli nationalists, much of the destructive intent is fueled by a mixture of nationalist politics, messianic longing, and the search for

Open Letter

to the Prime Minister

and People of Israel

The Imprisonment of Religious Israelis

Thursday, March 10, witnessed a great setback to religious freedom in Israel — and throughout the world.

We refer to the jailing of earnest, faithful sons of Israel — whose only crime was to try to pray upon the most sacred site of Judaism, the Temple Mount:

> *Our Father which art in heaven: Guard the children of all*
> *nations who perform thy will and fear they great name.*

We, as evangelical Christians, find the imprisonment of these sons of Israel within the gates of Jerusalem, biblically unconscionable.

This comes as an international shock to vast segments of the Evangelical world. For the Jewish people to be restricted and imprisoned for such a noble design staggers the moral imagination.

Exclusive and erroneous Islamic claims to this most holy site, militate against historical and biblical injunction. The People of Israel, through Abraham, Isaac, Jacob, David, Solomon, Ezra, Nehemiah, Haggai, Zechariah, and the early church (Stephen, Paul, James and Jesus Himself) with many others, paid the most holy price for this sanctified space. **The Almighty desires it to be a House of Prayer for all peoples.** (Isaiah 56:7)

If the sons and daughters of Zion are restricted access to Zion's holy hill, then the return of His chosen people to their land of promise is in vain — for the heart of Jerusalem awaits the foot of the Jew, not the trodding down by the gentiles.

Mr. Prime Minister, your brethren have **considered their ways** and gone up to the Mountain of the Lord. Therefore, we ask you to intervene on behalf of Israel's faithful who demonstrate their divine privilege. Your people, who gave to the gentiles the knowledge of the one true God, must be allowed full freedom of worship within the holy boundaries of the Mount.

May the Almighty strengthen the resolve of your government to do that which is right in the sight of the Lord.

> *... and the gentiles shall come to Thy light*
> *and kings to the brightness of Thy rising...*
> *the forces of the gentiles shall come unto Thee*
> *... they shall come up with acceptance on mine altar,*
> *and I will glorify the house of my glory.*
>
> (Isaiah 60)

Be strong, Mr. Prime Minister, and *"all ye people of Eretz Israel,' saith the Lord, "and work; for I am with you', saith the Lord of Hosts"*.

(Haggai 2:4)

Your Evangelical Friends in America

Conmittee of Concerned Evangelicals for Freedom of Worship on the Temple Mount

P.O. Box 6081   Norman, Oklahoma 73070
Terry Risenhoover   Dr. James DeLoach
                              Doug Krieger
                              Co-Chairmen

The Feast of Freedom — Pessah, 1983 (5743)

roots. In fact, some of the current extremism is a direct outgrowth of the ancient forecast of the Apocalypse.

The targets of the most spectacular incidents over the past months have been the Muslim authorities and the area they control in Jerusalem, but for the most part the people who planned or participated in the attacks are the violent fringe of an informal movement that stretches from the United States to the Middle East, and encompasses millions of evangelical Christians as well as some Israeli Jews. This unlikely coalition rests upon a common belief that the Final Days are upon us.[2]

Others have written about this plot or "conspiracy" between Christian and Jewish forces to build a Third Temple. The Jerusalem *Post* ran a special supplement on September 30, 1983 about the Temple Mount. One of the articles in the supplement, entitled "The Christian Connection," had this to say:

While Gush Emunim, Yeshivat Ateret Cohanim and other Jewish groups cast their eyes in the direction of the Temple Mount, evangelical Christians abroad are digging into their pockets to help things along.

So far, the Christian Community's support for the construction of the Third Temple has been somewhat discreet. But there are growing numbers of Christians, many organized into small churches and larger groups, who see the construction of a Third Temple as the cornerstone of their beliefs.

These are evangelical or Pentecostal Christians who believe the prophecies in the Hebrew Bible and the New Testament indicate that the building of the Third Temple on the Temple Mount is part of a divine plan leading up to the end of days.

Though there is a clear divergence in religious belief between these Christians and Jews who work towards the rebuilding of the Temple, they willingly and enthusiastically cooperate. Indeed, the Christians are encouraged by their leaders to contribute towards such groups as the Jerusalem Temple Foundation.

Such a view was stated by Stanley Goldfoot, activist and "foreign minister" of the Faithful of the Temple Mount who, in an earlier interview said, "I tell them there is no dialogue. I make it clear that I can't accept their views and they can't accept mine. If they are prepared to help us openly, then we're prepared to accept it."[3]

A periodical entitled *The Link,* commented:

> Two violent attempts to "liberate" the Temple Mount
> recently have taken place. . . According to Middle East
> correspondent Grace Halsell, "Increasingly Zionist
> fanatics—Israelis and Americans—are plotting to destroy
> Islam's sacred Al-Aqsa Mosque and the Dome of the Rock
> in Jerusalem. It is said that many of Israel's highest
> officials sanction Zionist plans to destroy the mosque,
> the site from whence Muhammad ascended into heaven,
> and to build a Jewish temple there.
>
> Christian Zionists, uncritical of any action undertaken
> by the Israeli government, apparently have the same
> rationale for supporting such actions.[4]

There was the charge that evangelical "Christians"
from Texas provided money for legal fees of those arrested
for the March 10, 1983 assault on the Mount. These
"Christian" sources were also alleged to have funded the
Lifta Band who had attempted to blow up the Dome of the
Rock and Al Aqsa Mosque in 1984.[5] If these allegations are
true, then these "Christians" should be condemned in the
strongest of terms.

Too often, evangelical Christians are all lumped
together by the press. This is unfortunate. The small group
of "Christians" who may have supported violent acts
toward the Moslem holy sites do not represent the
majority of believers.

Disinformation and Wrong Information

Disinformation as well as wrong information continue
to appear in the press concerning Christians and the
Temple Mount. The Jerusalem *Post* reported:

> . . . recently the Syrians have tried to make their mark by
> taking new directions. They have taken aim at Christians
> who support Israel. They have made a particular target
> the International Christian Embassy in Jerusalem,
> which represents in its own telling way the many
> millions of Evangelical Christians around the world.
>
> Thus in a recent issue of the Syrian Times, the Rev, Jan
> Willen van der Hoeven, one of the prominent leaders of
> the embassy was accused of telling the Jerusalem Post
> that "he believes in rebuilding the Temple on the debris of
> the holy al-Aqsa Mosque."

That Rev. van der Hoeven told the *Post* in an interview just the opposite proved no obstacle for the propagandists in Damascus.

The Syrians are evidently so disturbed by such "Biblical Christians" who have lent their support to Israel, that they are prepared to malign them and distort their views.[6]

Summary

The evangelical Christians are the "wild card" in the struggle of Jews against their fellow countrymen, their own political system, and the world of Islam. The evangelical Christian community, particularly in America, gives wide-spread support for Israel. This support includes finances as well as lobbying. They have, however, strongly condemned any violent attempt to destroy Moslem holy sites. Encouraging or funding this type of endeavor is inconsistent with the teachings of Scripture. Funding or helping to build a Third Temple is also something in which Christians should not participate.

The Christian community, however, has provided assistance in a legitimate matter, the scientific research in the mystery of the Temple's actual location.

Endnotes

1. See our comments in Chapter Thirteen.

2. Barbara and Michael Ledeen, "The Temple Mount Plot," *The New Republic*, June 18, 1984.

3. Haim Shapiro, The Christian Connection, Jerusalem *Post* Local Supplement September 30, 1983.

4. O. Kelly Ingram, *The Link* , November, 1983, p. 9.

5. Ledeen and Ledeen, ibid. p. 20.

6. Jerusalem *Post*, March 19, 1985.

CHAPTER NINE

WHERE DID THE TEMPLE
ACTUALLY STAND?

No other place in the world has inspired such zealous
activity for over 3,000 years. No other place in the world
has had so much written about it—barbs of ridicule as well
as songs of praise. No other place in the world has been so
closely studied and scrutinized as Jerusalem, so that
hardly a month goes by without at least one research
paper being published on one aspect or another of the
Temple Mount. Nevertheless, despite all that has been
written and done, a multitude of secrets still lay hidden in
the belly of the earth.[1]

As if there were not enough controversies surrounding
the Temple Mount the exact location of where the First and
Second Temple stood is now being hotly debated.
Throughout recent history most scholars have assumed
that the Dome of the Rock shrine was built over the
location of the First and Second Temple. Beneath the Dome
is a rock-mass known to the Moslems as *as-Sakhra.* This
rock-mass is the highest point on the Temple Mount.
Because this golden Dome was purposely erected over this
rock-mass it seemed logical to conclude that that is where
the Temples stood.

Archaeologists have not been able to find any trace of
the walls, gates or furniture of the Second Temple. One
hundred years ago Jerusalem explorer Charles Warren
declared, "We want to know where the Temple was."[2]

Archaeologist Kathleen Kenyon more recently wrote,
"Absolutely nothing survives of the temple built by
Herod."[3]

The same thought was echoed by the famous authority
on ancient Jerusalem, M. Avi-Yonah:

We know little more about the Temple Mount than
Warren did a century ago. The location of the actual
Temple, the central problem, cannot yet be ascertained.[4]

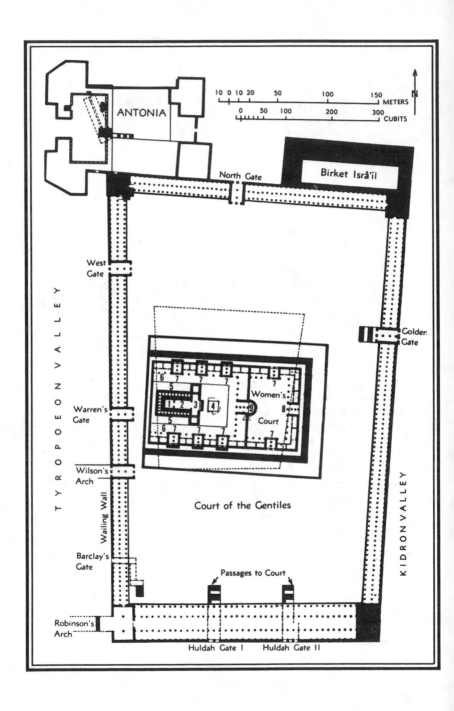

The authors Chuck Missler (left) and Don Stewart (right) standing on the Mount of Olives with the Dome of the Rock in the background (April 1991).

Lambert Dolphin and Robert Pendergraf working with wall radar in the 1983 SRI expedition in Israel.

Don Stewart and Robert Pendergraf working with a seismic sounder in the 1983 SRI expedition in Israel.

Aerial shot of the Temple Mount.

Don Stewart (left) and Chuck Missler (right) receiving an autographed limited edition of a work from Dr. Asher Kaufman.

Don Stewart, Asher Kaufman, and Chuck Missler on the Mount of Olives discussing the site of the Temple.

Asher Kaufman explaining where the priests lined up with the Holy of Holies from the Mount of Olives during the First Temple period.

Asher Kaufman explaining where the priests lined up with the Holy of Holies from the Mount of Olives during the Second Temple period.

Dome of the Tablets (Spirits) where Asher Kaufman believes the Holy of Holies stood in the First and Second Temple.

Closeup of the flat rock inside the Dome of the Tablets (Spirits) where the Ark of the Covenant may have rested during the First and Second Temple.

Authors reviewing ground penetrating radar plots of the Temple Mount.

El Kas Fountain, the site of the Holy of Holies according to the theory that the Temple stood between the Dome and Al Aqsa Mosque.

The authors at the Temple Institute in Jerusalem where implements have been made for use in the Third Temple. The actual implements intended for use are displayed in the photographs on the following pages (all photographs are used by permission of the Temple Institute).

Picture of the Temple Mount with the Dome of the Rock and Al Aqsa Mosque airbrushed out and a Third Temple put in their place.

Chuck Missler photographing the Temple implements at the Temple Institute in Jerusalem.

Don Stewart holding three pronged fork used to turn offerings on altar.
Next to him are the High Priests garments and copper wash basin.

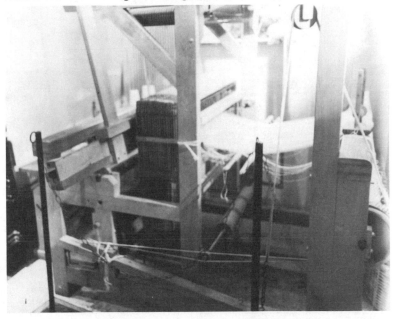

Semi-computerized loom on which the priestly garments are woven.

A copper psakhter where ashes of the outer offering were placed.

Silver trumpets, a symbol of the return to Zion.

(Top left) harp, (top right) lyre, (center) shofar or ram's horn, (bottom) measuring cups.

Silver Mizrak that caught the blood from the sacrifice and carried it to the altar.

Incense set (copper tray, silver chalice, silver ring, and cloth covering).

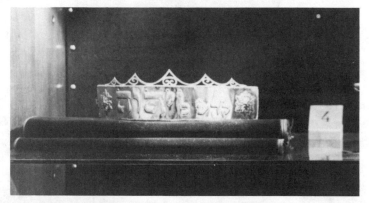

The pure gold diadem of the High Priest worn from ear to ear across his forehead and fastened with a thread of a tchelet.

Incense spices

Don Stewart and Temple Institute worker holding the shofar (ram's horn).

Temple Institute worker holding High Priests lottery box containing two lots: one marked for God and the other to the scapegoat.

A child's drawing on a wall in East Jerusalem where the Dome of the Rock (rt) is joined with the sacred Ka' aba in Mecca. This illustrates the reverence and respect that Moslems hold for the Dome as they equate it with their holiest site.

Since the Temple Mount is under Moslem control any archaeological work to determine where the Temple of the Jews stood is presently out of the question.

Dr. Asher Kaufman

In 1974, Dr. Asher Kaufman, a plasma physicist at the Rachah Institute in Jerusalem and an observant Jew, began to explore the subject of the original location of the Temple. According to Jewish Law, no Orthodox Jew is allowed to walk on the Temple Mount for fear he might accidentally walk upon the Holy of Holies. This rule seemed to keep Dr. Kaufman from making a first-hand examination of the Mount. However, he discovered that a non-priest could walk upon the area if he were considered to be cleaning, repairing or rebuilding the Temple. Though the rebuilding for him was purely theoretical, this allowed him to walk upon the Temple Mount and do his research.

Kaufman's approach combined a number of methods. These included the study of ancient Jewish sources which describe the Temple, its vicinity and its rituals. He also applied techniques from the modern science of measurement and astronomical observations as well as on site inspection.

In 1977 Kaufman wrote:

An air of mystery surrounds the Second Temple in Jerusalem. Where was it situated in the Temple area (Haram ash-Sharif)? What did it look like? For generations, scholars in general, clergy, archaeologists, engineers and historians have attempted to answer these two questions. The rock as-Sakhra in the Dome of the Rock plays a central role in the vast majority of these deliberations. It is regarded as the site either of the Holy of Holies or of the Altar of Sacrifice. A third question—is there any visible sign of the Temple today?—was answered by Simons (1952, p. 435) in the negative: "In contrast, however, with the principal monument of ancient Athens the buildings within the sacred precincts at Jerusalem have utterly disappeared."[5]

Dr. Kaufman's research has led him to a startling conclusion; the Foundation stone of the Temple is not the Dome of the Rock but another smaller protrusion of stone some 330 feet in the northwest corner of the compound. The site has a small cupola know as the "Dome of the Spirits" or "Dome of the Tablets." Kaufman further wrote:

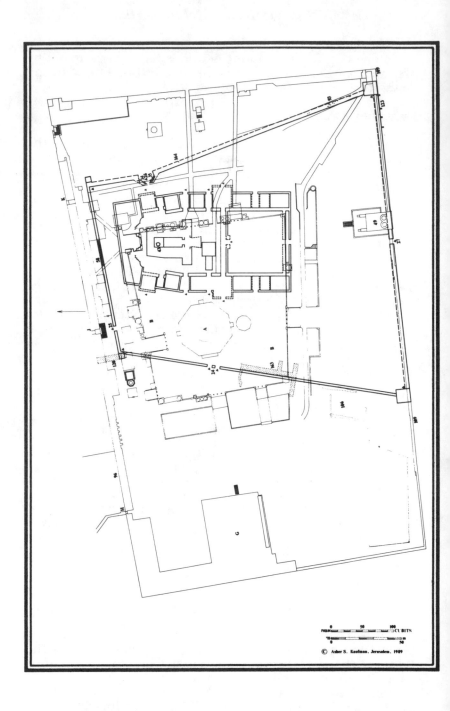

© Asher S. Kaufman, Jerusalem, 1989

It is almost axiomatic among scholars that no trace of the Jewish Temple is to be found on Jerusalem's Temple Mount . . . Despite this scholarly consensus, there *are*, however, traces of remains—a line of stones, a worked rock-mass, a cistern—and these ancient relics are sufficient, when added to the literary sources to locate the Second Temple, and even to trace out the First Temple, on the Temple Mount.

One of the most surprising conclusions from this evidence is that the golden Dome of the Rock in the middle of the Temple Mount was *not* built on the site of the Temple but to the south of it. The Original Temple site is approximately 330 feet (100 meters) to the northwest of the Dome of the Rock.[6]

Dome of the Spirits

About the Dome of the Tablets or Dome of the Spirits, Kaufman stated:

In Arabic this cupola is called Qubbat el-Arwah, Dome of the Spirits. Has this Arabic name preserved an ancient memory of the holiness of the site? In Sinai, where the glory of the Lord appeared before the whole community of Israel, Moses and Aaron addressed the Lord as "God of the spirits of all mankind" (Numbers 16:22; see also Numbers 27:16, Ezekiel 37, Job 12:10). Dome of the Spirits is certainly an appropriate name to mark the dwelling place of the Lord's name, the center of his Divine presence.[7]

The biblical basis for this name is possibly found in two passages in the Old Testament:

Then they fell on their faces and said, "O God, the God of the spirits of all flesh, shall one man sin, and You be angry with the congregation" . . . "Let the Lord, the God of the spirits of all flesh, set a man over the congregation" (Numbers 16:22;27:16).

Kaufman continues:

But this cupola has another Arabic name: Qubbat el-Alouah, Dome of the Tablets. In the Holy of Holies of Solomon's Temple was kept the Ark of the Covenant, now lost, containing the two stone Tablets of the law given to Moses on Mount Sinai. According to M. de Vogue, the name Dome of the Tablets was given to this cupola because it is dedicated to the memory of the Tablets of the

Law. Once more a name preserves the ancient memory of the location of the Holy of Holies.[8]

Bagatti's Work

Kaufman built upon the earlier work of Franciscan scholar Bellarmino Bagatti. Bagatti's research had lead him to the conclusion that the Dome of the Rock was not the site of the First and Second Temple. Though Bagatti rejected the Dome of the Rock as the actual site, he did not attempt to provide an alternative site. Dr. Kaufman commented on Bagatti's research:

> Bagatti offers no detailed solution of his own to the problem of the Temple's placement, other than saying at one point, that 'one is [thus] led to believe that the Temple was situated near the present-day El-Aqsa Mosque', that is, on the southern side of the Temple area . . .
> . . . Bagatti likewise rejects the identification of the rock as-Sakhra as the original location of the Temple. His argumentation against as-Sakhra as the original location of the Altar of Sacrifice is a forceful one. . . he reasons that if the Altar had occupied that site, the steep slope to the west of it would have necessitated the construction of a massive infrastructure to support the Hekhal (Sanctuary), which stood to the west of the Altar. However, there is absolutely no evidence of such a structure.[9]

Kaufman has traced the tradition of the Dome being built on the Temple site back to the seventh century A.D. It has been accepted by Christians, Jews, and Moslems as the actual site. The *Jewish Encyclopedia* said:

> The most probable site of the Temple is just west of the "Dome of the Rock" in the center of the Mosque of Omar. The bronze altar was probably built upon this rock. The mosque was built over a rock the traditions of which are sacred; probably the site was the same as that of the temple which Hadrian erected to Jupiter. This in turn was the site of Herod's temple, which would naturally be that of Solomon's. The persistency of sacred sites in the East makes this most likely.[10]

The Evidence

The evidence for Kaufman's hypothesis are many. There is the problem with the traditional site of the Dome of the Rock as well as evidence that the Temple stood elsewhere.

There are several problems that Kaufman mentions concerning the Dome of the Rock (as-Sakhra) as the traditional site:

> Scholars who accept as-Sakhra as the site of the Temple, however, are divided about its role within the Temple precincts. Some have speculated that this rock-mass marks the place of the Holy of Holies, the most sacred chamber of the Temple . . . This location of the Temple has been criticized on several grounds. For one, when the Temple plan is laid out on the Temple Mount according to this location of the Holy of Holies, there is very little room between the eastern wall of the Temple and the eastern outer wall of the Temple Mount. This contradicts the Misnah (Middot 2:1), the most important literary source about the Temple; the Mishnah states that the greater part of the Outer Court (Har Habbayit) was on the south; the next greater, on the east; next, that on the north; and the smallest part on the west. This description in the Misnah makes it difficult to locate the Holy of Holies at as-Sakhra.[11]

The Golden Gate

As far as the Bible is concerned, the Golden Gate is the most important of all the gates in Jerusalem. It is the only gate that leads directly to the Temple Mount from the Mount of Olives.

Beneath the present Golden Gate, built during the Turkish rule of Jerusalem, an older gate has recently been discovered. In 1969 Archaeologist James Fleming was investigating the present Golden Gate when he fell into a deep hole. Heavy rains had made the area damp and the ground gave way beneath his feet. Fleming found himself in a hole eight foot deep where he was knee-deep in bones. What he saw was the remnants of an ancient double arched gate:

> Then I noticed with astonishment that on the eastern face of the turret wall, directly beneath the Golden Gate itself, were five wedge-shaped stones neatly set up in a massive arch spanning the turret wall. Here were the remains of an earlier gate to Jerusalem, below the Golden Gate, one that apparently had never been fully documented.[12]

Asher Kaufman believes Fleming's discovery provided further evidence as to the site of the Temple:

The Second Temple, as well as Solomon's Temple before it, faced east; that is, it was entered from the east. The only clearly visible entrance to the Temple Mount from the east is through the blocked Golden Gate. One would expect this entrance to the Temple Mount to be opposite the entrance to the Temple—in mid-position of the Temple Mount if the Temple had stood where the Dome of the Rock now stands. This expectation is strengthened by the many messianic associations with this eastern gate to the Temple Mount. It is the gate of mercy, of judgment. It is the gate through which the Messiah will pass when the great day comes.

Strangely enough, the Golden Gate is *not* positioned midway in the eastern wall of the Temple Mount; the Golden Gate would not lead directly to a temple placed on the site of the Dome of the Rock. Indeed, the mid-point of the Golden Gate is located about 348 feet (106 meters) north of the line running through the center of the Dome of the Rock in an east-west direction. This fact, of course, consistent with the placement of the Temple north of the Dome of the Rock, in the northern part of the Temple Mount. Moreover, it now seems clear that before the Golden Gate was constructed, the entrance to the Temple Mount from outside the city was in exactly the same location. Recently, part of an arch was discovered directly beneath the Golden Gate. This partial arch definitely belongs to an older gate, a gate that may date even to Solomonic times.[13]

Kaufman comments on the significance of the Golden Gate with the location of the Temple:

The Temple was built in a large measure according to a symmetrical plan (see, for example, Middot 4[7], 2[5], 1[4]). One may, therefore, specify an axis of symmetry. The verse about the red heifer (Numbers 19:4), " . . . and he shall sprinkle of its blood *opposite* the front of the Tent of Meeting seven times," can be interpreted to mean that, during the sprinkling of blood at the time of the Second Temple, the priest stood on an imaginary straight line which was the continuation eastward of the axis of symmetry. The ceremony as recorded in Middot 2[4] took the following form— "All the walls that were there were high except the eastern wall, so that the priest who burnt the red heifer might, while standing on the Mount of Olives by directing his gaze carefully, see the entrance of the Hekhal at the time of the sprinkling of the blood." He must have chosen a high spot on the Mount. For one reason, the Temple was also built as a fortress and there would have been great reluctance to lower the Eastern wall more than was necessary. The Mount of Olives is flat-topped and·so in order to see into the Temple, the priest would have to stand on the western side of the flat-topped area, for example, that circumscribed by the contour line of 800 m.

In itself, the observation by the priest is insufficient to locate the position of the Temple. However, if it is combined with the condition that the Temple axis was aligned exactly or approximately in the east-west direction, the northern and southern limits to the position of the axis can be approximately defined.

The conclusion to be drawn is that the axis was in the northern part of the Temple area.[14]

Threshing Floor

The Bible says that the Altar of Sacrifice was built over a threshing floor. Yet the "sacred" rock, over which the Dome of the Rock was built, would not have made a good threshing floor. Kaufman wrote:

However, the general character of the rock is not consistent with a good threshing floor, especially in the case of Araunah (Ornan), oxen were being used in the threshing process (II Samuel 24:22). Their legs would have been endangered in encountering the irregular and sloping surface of al-Sakhra.[15]

Where the Ark Rested

Kaufman concludes that the Ark of the Covenant rested on the flat rock covered by the Dome of the Spirits:

The conclusion, therefore, is that the actual Ark of the Covenant, which the people of Israel carried through the desert to the Promised Land, rested on the exposed bedrock sheltered by the unassuming cupola known as the Dome of the Tablets! Thus this bedrock is one of the most authentically preserved remnants of a sacred past that has survived to the present day—the podium of the holiest enclave within the holiest building in Israel's history, the actual stone on which the Ark of the Covenant rested.[16]

Divine Providence?

Kaufman believes that Divine Providence has led him to his present conclusions:

> The picture of the Second Temple that has been pieced together from archaeological and other sources is no longer a mere sketch; rather it approaches the architectural plan of an actual building. And, most importantly, it would appear that Divine Providence has ensured that no major structure occupy the actual site of the Temple . . . the magnificent Dome of the Rock, stands south of the Temple site. Does this fact, together with the Jewish return to the Land, augur the Latter Days prophesied by Isaiah (56:7): "And I shall bring them to My holy mountain . . . for My house shall be called a house of prayer for all peoples."[17]

Evidence Covered Up

One of the disturbing things about the present situation is that the evidence that is on the surface has been covered up. Kaufman writes:

> All signs of rock-mass 1 are buried beneath a new garden and wall recently built by Moslem authorities . . . Despite its great importance to solving the problem of the First and Second Temple, this large rock-mass can no longer be studied by scholars.[18]

In 1970, as the Moslems were digging a pit, a row of stones were discovered that revealed an ancient wall. Dr. Ze'ev Yeivin was called to the scene and arrived to make some quick drawings. Kaufman believes the wall Yeiven saw belonged to the compound of the Second Temple:

> The wall Yeivin had seen was the foundation of the eastern wall of the Second Temple Compound itself.[19]

When Yeivin returned a week later, the wall had been demolished and the stones removed.

> We are also told that the Moslem authorities removed the ancient remains before they could be fully examined, drawn and recorded, and apparently before they were photographed. These ancient remains . . . have thus been destroyed forever without any adequate record having been made for scholar's use now or in the future.[20]

There seems to be a deliberate attempt to destroy any evidence of a past Jewish presence on the Temple Mount. Asher Kaufman listed 16 different Jewish antiquities that were destroyed by the Waqf in recent years or buried under dirt and concrete.

Dan Bahat, archaeologist for the Jerusalem Ministry of Education investigated the charges of alteration of Jewish antiquities on the Temple Mount complex. Bahat told the daily paper *Ha'aretz* that he confirmed Kaufman's findings and added a list of other changes. These included the burial of the remains of the Northern Wall of the outer courtyard of the First Temple, and the burial of the Temple basins from the Herodian period.

Bahat also reported that the remains of part of the Western Wall of the Temple Mount is covered by meters of dirt.

In June 1979, in order to dig a ditch, two walls were destroyed. These walls are believed to be the foundation of the Northern wall of the prayer area of the Second Temple, and the foundation of the Northern Wall of the Second Temple.

In addition, the Waqf sealed off beyond recognition one of the Hulda gates on the Southern Wall. The Hulda gates were used as entries to the Temple Mount during the Second Temple period. The Waqf also buried some of the adjoining steps and the ancient tiling.

Bahat emphasized that much of the work done on the sites is repairable yet damage has been done.

The Jerusalem *Post* wrote:

Remains of a wall said to contain Herodian-style stones were found on the Temple Mount 12 years ago— almost precisely where a controversial researcher places the eastern wall of Herod's Temple.

Knowledge of this wall—the first possible remains of the Jerusalem Temple ever uncovered—has been suppressed for the past decade because of its possible political implications. Although some scholars were aware of it, at least one of Israel's senior archaeologists heard about it for the first time in March 1980 from a reporter.

The Western Wall, the focus of Jewish prayer for centuries, is not a remnant of the Temple but of the massive wall supporting the Temple Mount.

The wall was uncovered in 1970 when the Supreme Moslem Council excavated a pit for water storage just off the northeast edge of the platform supporting the Dome of the Rock. A government archaeologist, who asked to remain anonymous, visited the site after being informed the ancient remains had been uncovered. He told the Jerusalem *Post* that he saw several courses of a massive wall, some of whose stones had the smooth margins typical of the Herodian stones seen in the Western Wall. By the time he returned with other archaeologists, however, the remains—five meters long, two meters thick and several courses high—had been knocked down. The archaeologist said he wrote a report on his find including sketches of the stones, but did not publish it. 'I just felt the matter was too sensitive,' he said. The sensitivity lay in the proximity of the Jews most holy site with the Islamic shrine.[21]

What was the Rock?

If the rock mass which the Dome of the Rock covers was not the place of the Altar of Sacrifice or the Holy of Holies in the First and Second Temple then what was it? Kaufman believes it might be the "Stone of the Claimants" where announcements of lost and found property were made.[22]

Changes in Due East?

In Dr. Asher Kaufman's article in BAR,[23] he was intrigued to perceive a 6° displacement between the alignments of the First and Second Temples. The First Temple appears to be aligned 6.2° north of what is presently due east. There was no particular explanation or conjecture for the difference in alignment of the two temples.

The 6° displacement from the east of the pre-exilic Temple has been the subject of numerous studies without any resolution.[24]

During one of our visits, in 1985, the authors called Dr. Kaufman's attention to the possibility that perhaps the direction of due east *changed* during the period of time between the two Temples.

All of the ancient calendars apparently required adjustment in 701 B.C., possibly due to energy transfers between the planet Mars and the Earth. Conjectures deriving from orbital mechanics studies between the Earth and Mars suggest that earlier resonance of the orbits of these two planets may have included energy transfers which changed the revolutions from 360 days and 720 days for the Earth and Mars, respectively, to 365 1/4 days and 687 days from a series of near pass-bys. In addition,

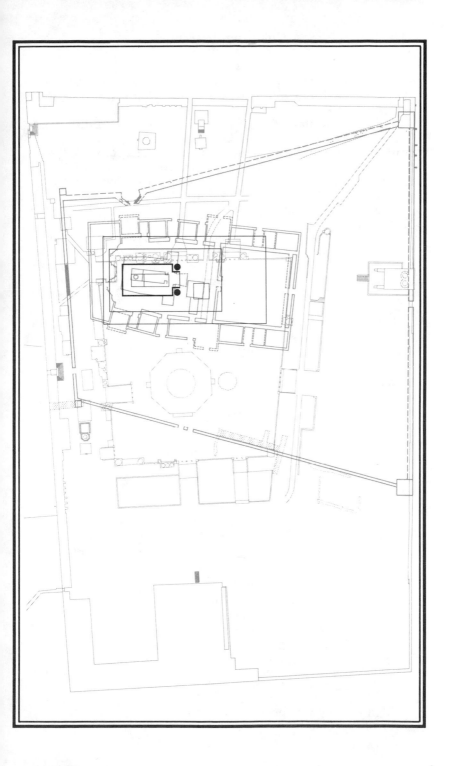

computer simulations suggest that the axis rotation may also have been effected with a change of about 6.5° in due east.[25]

The possibility of a near pass-by of the planet Mars may also have been documented in the writings of Jonathan Swift known as *Gulliver's Travels*.[26] Visiting the land of Laputa, Gulliver is confronted with the astronomers of Laputa who describe the two moons of Mars, and their motions, in remarkably precise detail.

Since Swift published his famous fantasy 151 years before the discovery of the two moons of Mars,[27] this implies that he may have been inadvertently relying on earlier records which he may have regarded as mythical, but were, in fact, eyewitness accounts. For someone on the earth to view the two moons of Mars with the naked eye, Mars would have to have been as close as 80,000 miles from the earth.

The apparent adjustment of 6.2° between the two Temples could be explained by this theory of the change in due east. Only time will tell if this is so.

Kaufman's Controversial Theory

Asher Kaufman's theory has generated international interest. As always, a new idea that upsets cherished time-honored traditions always runs into a lot of criticism. Asher Kaufman's proposal that the Temple site is different than originally believed is no exception. The Los Angeles *Times* reported the following:

> The theory of a Hebrew University physics professor that the foundation rock of the ancient Jerusalem temples is located 330 feet north of the traditionally accepted place remains a minority position among archaeologists despite the professor's recent article in the U.S. published Biblical Archeology Review. . .
>
> Kaufman has made the argument for a number of years, however, and a recently published book by Father Bellarmino Bagatti, a Franciscan scholar, repeats a similar claim he has been making since 1958.
>
> . . . An official of the Department of Antiquities here said that excavations in the Temple Mount area by Muslims, who have authority over the area under Israeli law, have been going on since about 1968.
>
> "They consider the Temple Mount as a holy site to them but do not consider that it is a holy site to others," the official said.

Archeology in Jerusalem is controversial by its very nature. Besides complaints that Muslim authorities are destroying evidence of Jewish and Christian sites-either by accident or on purpose-there are charges that Jewish archaeologists are trying to destroy evidence of Muslim use. UNESCO makes this charge regularly, and Israel rejects it just as regularly, saying that it is a symptom of United Nation's anti-Israel bias.[28]

The theories of Kaufman have also caused interest among Israeli archaeologists. The Jerusalem *Post* commented:

Reaction among Israeli archaeologists to Kaufman's theory—familiar to them from extensive conversations he has had with them over the years—ranges from almost total skepticism to interest and encouragement. Of eight interviewed, almost none dismissed it out of hand.

"Its a very interesting theory," says Ze'ev Yeiven, deputy director of the Antiquities Department. "But establishing it would require excavations in the area."

Prof. Nahman Avigad, who conducted the Jewish Quarter digs, was the most outspokenly sceptical. "I don't understand his theory, therefore I don't believe it." Avigad had not known of the wall remains discovered 16 years ago.

Professor Binyamin Mazar, who led nine years of excavations at the foot of the Temple Mount, declined to comment. "It's none of my business he said."

Dan Bahat challenged Kaufman's archaeological evidence, saying that there was no proof that the stone remains in the northern part of the Temple Mount, cited by the researcher as part of the Temple compound, were actually from the Second Temple period.

One of the country's outstanding archaeologists, who requested anonymity, praised Kaufman as a 'thorough man and straight—and that applies to his scientific approach.' However, he said, there were few facts to sustain the theory. 'It could be, but the evidence isn't strong enough.'

Meir Ben-Dov, who had been Mazar's deputy, also said that Kaufman had not proven his case but he agreed with the researcher that the Temple must have been north of the 'Dome of the Rock.' A similar opinion was expressed by another archaeologist although several others said they continued to believe in the 'Dome of the Rock' as the temple site.

Kaufman professed not to be disturbed by the reservations of the archaeologists, noting that his approach differed from the methodology. 'They've been trained to dig and ascribe dates according to layers. On the Temple Mount, where you can't dig, you have to rely on every possible piece of information.'29

Summary

Because of the current political situation, it is impossible to do any excavating on the Mount. Hence there is no consensus of opinion as to where the Temple originally stood. The Temple Mount is known to contain several dozen cisterns, underground passages and store rooms associated with the First and Second Temples. For historic reasons, completely apart from spiritual considerations, the location of the Temple should be known.

God may have ordained that no pagan structure would be built on the site of the Temple. When the Dome of the Rock was constructed the builders were possibly led to the site by Jews living in Jerusalem at that time. It is likely that they would have deliberately mislead their Moslem conquerors as to protect the sanctity of the genuine site.

However, the theory that the Temple was located north of the Dome of the Rock is not the only alternative to the traditional site.

Endnotes

1. Meir Ben Dov, *In the Shadow of the Temple*, Harper and Row Publishers, New York, 1982, p 77.

2. Charles Warren, Extracts from the report of the public meeting of the Palestine Exploration Fund, on June 11, 1868, p. 6.

3. Kathleen Kenyon, *Digging Up Jerusalem*, London, 1974.

4. M. Avi-Yonah, "Jerusalem of the Second Temple Period," in *Jerusalem Revealed*, The Israel Exploration Society and Shikmona, Jerusalem, 1975, p. 13.

5. Asher S. Kaufman, "New Light Upon Zion, The Plan and Precise Location of the Second Temple," Ariel, Number 43, Jerusalem, 1977, p. 63.

6. Asher S. Kaufman, "Where The Ancient Temple of Jerusalem Stood," Biblical Archeological Review, Vol IX No. 2, March/April 1983, p. 42.

7. Kaufman, BAR, p. 45.

8. Kaufman, BAR, p. 45.

9. Asher S. Kaufman, Christian News From Israel, 1979, pp. 55,57.

10. The Jewish Encyclopedia, Vol 6, p. 139.

11. Kaufman, BAR, p. 43.

12. James Fleming, "The Undisclosed Gate Beneath Jerusalem's Golden Gate," Biblical Archeology Review, January/February, 1983, p. 30.

13. Kaufman, BAR, p. 45.

14. Kaufman, Ariel, p. 68.

15. Asher S. Kaufman, "The Foundation Stone of the Temple," Unpublished paper.

16. Kaufman, BAR , p. 54.

17. Kaufman, Christian News From Israel, p. 57.

18. Kaufman, BAR , p. 49 (caption).

19. Kaufman, BAR , p. 44.

20. "Ancient Remains on the Temple Mount Must Not Be Destroyed," editorial, Biblical Archeological Review, Vol IX No. 2, March/April 1983, p. 60.

21. Jerusalem *Post*, April, 1983.

22. Kaufman, BAR, p. 53.

23. Kaufman BAR, p. 56.

24. H. Van Dyke, Palestine Exploration Quarterly, Jan-June 1978, 2 H.

25. The Earth apparently had an original orbit of 360 days. (Genesis 7:24, 8:34, etc.) Donald W. Patten, Ronald R. Hatch, Loren C. Steinhauer, *The Long Day of Joshua and Six Other Catastrophes*, Baker Book House, Grand Rapids, Michigan, 1973. Also, Chuck Missler, Signs in the Heavens, Koinonia House, P.O. Box 881, Big Bear Lake, CA 92315.

26. Jonathan Swift, *Gulliver's Travels*, Random House, New York, 1958, p. 134. Originally published in 1726.

27. The two moons of Mars are very small and have very little reflectivity (albedo). They were unknown to the astronomical world until discovered by Asaph Hall in 1877. At the U.S. Naval Observatory. Swift published his book in 1726.

28. Los Angeles *Times*, Saturday March 5, 1983.

29. Abraham Rabinovich, The Jerusalem *Post*, August 9, 1983.

CHAPTER TEN

DID THE TEMPLE STAND TO THE SOUTH OF THE DOME?

The traditional site of the Temple has been the rock over which the Dome of the Rock was built. Most people still accept this idea. Recently Asher Kaufman has gained international attention by proposing that the Temple stood 106 meters to the north of the Dome. It is possible that neither of these sites are correct. There is the possibility that the Temple actually stood to the south of the Dome of the Rock.

There have been those in times past who have argued that the Temple was actually south of the Dome of the Rock, between it and the Al Aqsa Mosque. The Jewish Encyclopedia says:

> There can be no doubt that the Temple of Solomon was situated upon the more easterly of the two hills which form the present Haram area in Jerusalem, in the center of which is the Mosque of Omar. Fergusson, Trupp, Lewin and W.R. Smith held that the Temple was built in the southwest corner of the present Haram area: but this view is false. That site is a part of an artificial extension of the level of the Temple area over the Tyropeon valley and probably was not made before the time of Herod.[1]

Recent Research

Recent research, however, may lend more credibility to the southern hypothesis. Amidst the numerous controversies regarding the location of the First and Second Temples, it is interesting that some of the earliest theories involved the area south of the Dome of the Rock, in the direction of the Al Aqsa Mosque.

Bellarmino Bagatti, the man who stirred Asher Kaufman on his quest, not only cast doubts about the Dome of the Rock as the site of the First and Second Temples, he also believed that the actual site was on the southern side of the Dome, near the Al Aqsa Mosque.

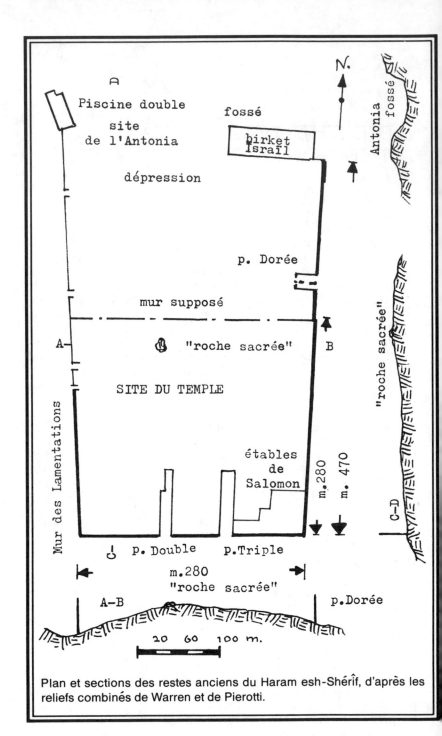

Plan et sections des restes anciens du Haram esh-Shérîf, d'après les reliefs combinés de Warren et de Pierotti.

Current conjectures concerning the possible southern location are based on a number of considerations.

The Topography

Despite the many traditions and legends surrounding the Temple Mount, it may surprise the reader to discover that the offering of Isaac by Abraham[2] may have no direct connection to the Temple Mount.

The Temple Mount is part of a ridge system broadly known as "Mount Moriah," which begins at the City of David to the south, and gradually increases in elevation as it meanders northward. The Temple Mount itself is not at the highest peak of this ridge system.

The Temple Mount is about 741 meters above sea level; the highest point on the ridge is over 770 meters above sea level, slightly further to the north. (See topographical map on page 148).

In over 100 places in the Old Testament, God prohibited placing a worship site on the "high places."[3] If Solomon's Temple would have been built at the peak, it would have been inconsistent with God's established pattern of worship.

As Abraham offered his son Isaac at the top of Mount Moriah, many believe it would have been on the highest part of the Mount which is even further northward than the present Temple Mount itself. It is amazing that 2000 years later, another Father offered his only beloved son as an offering on that very spot. Abraham apparently realized that he was acting out a prophecy since he named the place Yahweh-Yireh, "In the mount of the Lord, it shall be provided."[4]

The peak is a place which, at the time of Herod's Temple, was outside of the city wall to the north and it had a striking similarity to a "skull"—a place called Golgatha. That spot of humiliation can still be seen today, overlooking the unsightly Sha'ar Shekhem bus station.

Computer Models

The Old Testament (the Tanach), the Mishna and the writings of Flavius Josephus, record various sightings of activities within the Temple Courts from certain vantage points outside the Temple area. Specifically, both Herod Agrippa, and the Roman Conqueror Titus Vespasian, are recorded as being able to see into the Temple Courts from their respective ramparts.

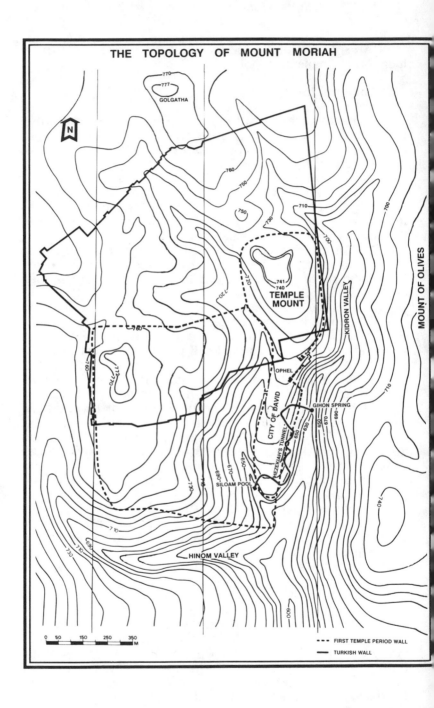

THE TOPOLOGY OF MOUNT MORIAH

GOLGATHA

TEMPLE MOUNT

KIDRON VALLEY

MOUNT OF OLIVES

OPHEL

GIHON SPRING

CITY OF DAVID

HEZEKIAH'S TUNNEL

SILOAM POOL

HINOM VALLEY

0 50 150 250 350
M

- - - FIRST TEMPLE PERIOD WALL

——— TURKISH WALL

Three-dimensional computer models of the Temple have been programmed and attempts have been made to reconcile these sightings with the topography of the Temple Mount area.[5] These studies suggest that the Temple appears to have been located at a lower elevation on the Mount area.

Since the ridge system in the area of the Temple Mount rises northward, a lower elevation is suggestive of a more southerly location. While not conclusive, these studies have encouraged the exploration of additional evidences of a southward possibility.

The Roman Temple of Aelia Capitolina

Perhaps the most provocative insight emerges from considerations of the Roman architecture of the period. Emperor Hadrian visited Jerusalem in A.D. 129, and apparently gave a preliminary approval for the rebuilding of the temple.

An uproar involving the Samaritans caused him to renege on this approval.[6] In any case, in A.D. 132, the famous Bar Kochba revolt erupted. It enjoyed a brief success for a little over three years (132-135). During their brief control of the Temple Mount, the reconstruction of a Third Temple was probably begun.[7]

The Romans eventually crushed the revolt and, in their exasperation in administering this troublesome province, they determined to eliminate further disturbances by establishing the Roman city Aelia Capitolina to replace Jerusalem and destroying all evidences of the earlier Jewish temples by constructing their own edifices on the temple site. This is of particular interest since they obviously knew the true location at that time.

The name "Aelia Capitolina" was composed of two elements: "Aelia" after the Emperor himself, whose full name was Publius Aelius Hadrianus; and "Capitolina" after the three deities appointed to be the patrons of the new city, the Capitolina triad: Jupiter, Juno and Minerva. The worship of these deities was to be instituted in a temple erected in their honor on the Temple Mount.

Roman Architectural Practice

During that period the prevailing trend in Roman architectural style featured a rectangular main temple facing a polygon structure with a large courtyard area between them. The rectangular basilica served as the

Baalbek: Axonometric View

Baalbek: Plan View

1) Temple of Jupiter
2) Forecourt
3) Sacrificial Altar
4) Hexagonal Forecourt and Propylaea
5) Temple of Dionysus (Bacchus)

temple proper, with the polygonal structure serving variously as a rotunda, meeting place, or, in some cases, as a mausoleum.[8]

A dramatic example of this architecture has been discovered in the Temple to Jupiter at Baalbek, Lebanon.[9]

Significantly, this temple also was in honor of a triad of deities: Jupiter, Venus and Mercury. What makes this structure so provocative is that if this Roman temple plan is overlaid on the Temple Mount, it matches the Al Aqsa Mosque and the Dome of the Rock! The Temple of Jupiter at Baalbek involved a hexagon rather than an octagon, but the similarity, in fact, the congruence, of the design is most striking (see figure on page 150).

This shouldn't be too surprising since both the temple of Aelia Capitolina and the temple at Baalbek were built about the same time, A.D 138-161,[10] and they were both built by the same sponsor: Antoninus Pius, to honor Hadrian, his predecessor and benefactor. It would seem that the subsequent destruction of the Roman buildings on the Temple Mount over the following centuries left the base of ruins that were probably subsequently adapted for Byzantine churches, which, in turn, were the foundations for the Moslem construction five centuries later.

The Moslem Structures

The Dome of the Rock was built by Abd-al-Malik and the Al Aqsa Mosque was built as a stone structure by his son and heir, al-Walid (705-715.)[11] The two structures were probably a derivative of Byzantine-Christian architecture.

The original Al Aqsa Mosque was considerably larger than the present structure.[12] Its plan resembled that of a basilica, borrowed from Christian architecture and adapted to the needs of the Moslem prayer rite.

As Moslem buildings go, the Dome of the Rock is entirely unique. The Dome of the Rock appears to have been adapted from a commemorative church, such as the octagonal church built by the Byzantines on top of Mount Gerizim after suppressing the revolt of the Samaritans in the sixth century.[13]

Thus, it appears that both the Al Aqsa Mosque and the Dome of the Rock may have been built upon the ruins of Byzantine structures which were themselves built on the original Roman foundations, battered by the centuries of conquest and re-conquest.

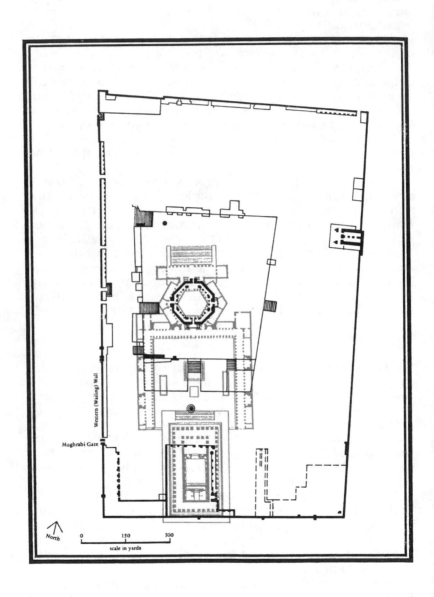

Western (Wailing) Wall

Moghrabi Gate

North

0   150   300

scale in yards

The Equestrian Statue

As part of the Roman temple complex, an equestrian statue of Hadrian, the builder's predecessor and benefactor, was placed in the large courtyard between the rectangular temple and the polygon structure (see the diagram on page 152).

Jerome makes reference to this statue as being directly over the very site of the Holy of Holies.[14] This would suggest that the Holy of Holies was in the vicinity of Al-Kas, the washing fountain which is presently seen between the Al Aqsa Mosque and the Dome of the Rock.

Three Potential Coincidences

If it turns out that this southern conjecture is the correct location of the First and Second Temples, several fascinating ironies are suggested. If this proves to be correct, the tradition of praying at the Western ("Wailing") Wall is at the very location that is as close to the Holy of Holies as one could approach without having direct access to the Temple Mount itself.

Prophetic irony also emerges from Daniel chapter nine. In Daniel 9:24-27, the angel Gabriel tells Daniel that after the Messiah is executed,[15] "the people of the prince that shall come shall destroy the city and the sanctuary." This prophecy was fulfilled when the Roman legions destroyed Jerusalem and the Temple in A.D. 70. Is it possible that "the people of the Prince that shall come"—the Romans—may have inadvertently documented the very site of the Temple which they were trying to obliterate?

This would also involve an additional irony since it is that very "Prince that shall come" who is destined to desecrate this coming Temple in his final hours.[16] (This is discussed in Chapter Twelve).

The Hidden Chambers

The records of Josephus also mention several priests who negotiated their freedom during the Roman scourge of A.D. 70 by bartering various temple implements.[17] If these priests had access to some of these items, this implies that other items may also be hidden in secret chambers somewhere under the Mount. This seems to substantiate the widely held view that the actual temple implements—perhaps even the Ark of the Covenant itself—are still hidden somewhere under the Temple Mount.

The possibility of uncovering these treasures is exciting and some of the technologies which may prove useful in this quest will be discussed in the next chapter.

Present State

The present state for the search of the Temple's location can be summed up as follows: The traditional site of the Temple is the Dome of the Rock. Most archaeologists, particularly in Israel, still hold that belief. Father Bellarmino Bagatti's research led him to believe that the Dome of the Rock was not the correct site. He suggested that the Temple originally stood on the southern side of the Mount near the present day Al Aqsa Mosque. Recent evidence lends some credence to this theory.

Dr. Asher Kaufman, building upon Bagatti's research, provides a large body of evidence that the Temple originally stood on the northern side of the Mount. Thus there are, at the very least, three possible sites as to where the Temple actually stood, and no one today knows which site is correct.

The Ultimate Resolution

How will these conflicting possibilities be resolved? There are experts and evidences on all sides. The numerous controversies about the Temple Mount are, of course, some of the most emotional and topical areas of current disputes in Israel. The very emergence of the Temple Mount in the national consciousness is, in itself, a provocative sign.

There are a number of advanced technologies that are non-invasive which can facilitate these investigations, and these will be discussed in the next chapter. However, the ultimate resolution clearly will require penetrating the Temple Mount itself, for it to relinquish its secrets.

It will take some truly remarkable leadership and persuasiveness to unravel the complex political barriers that presently block any such undertakings. Just such a leader may be about to emerge on the world scene.

Endnotes

1. Jewish Encyclopedia Judaica, vol. 6, pp. 113,114.

2. Genesis 22.

3. Total occurrences of "high places" is 97. Examples: Lev 26:30; Num 22:41; 33:52; Deu 33:29; 1 Ki 3:2,3; 12:31,32; 13:2,32-33; 14:23; 22:43; 2 Ki 12:3; 14:4; 15:4,35; 16:4; 17:9,11,29,32; 18:4,22; 21:3; 23:5,8,9,13,19,20; 2 Ch 11:15; 2 Ch 14:3,5; 15:17; 17:6; 20:33; 21:11; 28:4,25; 31:1; 32:12; 33:3,17,19; 34:3; Job 25:2; Psalm 78:58; Pro 8:2; 9:14; Isaiah 15:2; 36:7; Jer 3:2,21; 4:11; 7:29,31; 17:3; 19:5; Jer 32:35; 48:35; Eze 6:3,6; 16:16,39; 36:2; 43:7; Hos 10:8; Amos 4:13; Mic 1:3;3:12.

4. Genesis 22:14.

5. Some of these studies have been done by Tuvia Sagiv, a prominent Israeli architect in Tel Aviv, using Auto-CAD, a computer software system adapted for this purpose.

6. It appears that Hadrian had earlier granted permission for the rebuilding of the temple. (Chrysostom, "Orat. iii. in Judaeos", "Chron. Alex." 118 A.D.; Nicephorus, "Hist. Eccl.", iii.24; and Cedrenus, "Script. Byz." xii.249.) Subsequent problems with the Samaritans caused Hadrian to order the cessation of the building.

7. This is suggested in the several coins issued in the Bar Kokhba period. Encyclopedia Judaica, vol. 4, pp. 230,231.

8. The trend emphasizing spatial composition in Roman architecture climaxed under Trajan and Hadrian (98 - 138) and was continued by Antoninus Pius, Hadrian's successor. (Encyclopedia Britannica, Vol. 13, p. 971). See also references in the bibliography.

9. First discovered by a German expedition, 1898 - 1903. Palestine Exploration Fund, 1904, p. 58; 1905, p. 262.

10. Wood and Dawkins (1757) attribute this temple to Aelius Antoninus Pius who reigned A.D. 138-161. This temple is also represented on the reverse of several coins of the second and third centuries: Septimius Severus, Caracalla and others; the latest, Valerian.

11. The Christian pilgrim Bishop Arculf of France, who visited in about A.D. 680, related that a large house of prayer made of wood stood at the southern end of the Temple Mount. This was the earliest rendering of Al Aqsa.

12. The studies of K.A.C. Creswell, one of the great scholars of early Moslem architecture, and R. W. Hamilton highlight this. Meir Ben-Dov, *In the Shadow of the Temple*, Harper and Row Publishers, New York, 1982, p 77.

13. Recognizing this similarity of form, the nineteenth century scholar James Ferguson suggested that Abd-al-Malik's Dome of the Rock was essentially a Byzantine church that had been converted into a Moslem building.

14. Jerome, Commentary on Isaiah 2:9.

15. The prophecy in Daniel indicates that the Messiah appears after 69 "weeks" of years expire after the commandment to rebuild Jerusalem was given following the Babylonian Captivity. It also indicates that the Messiah will be "cut off" prior to the destruction of Jerusalem in A.D. 70 See Appendix 1).

16. Daniel 9:27.

17. Josephus, Jewish Wars, p, 228.

CHAPTER ELEVEN

ENTER MODERN SCIENCE

Though the original Temple was constructed some three thousand years ago it seems that modern science, apart from on site archaeology, may be able to solve the mystery of where it once stood. Despite the research of Asher Kaufman and others, the exact spot where the First and Second Temples is still uncertain.

This uncertainty is what generated the interest of the authors of this book to become involved in the quest for the actual Temple site. The authors were contacted by Lambert Dolphin, then Senior Research Physicist of the Science and Archaeology Laboratory of SRI International in Menlo Park, California.

SRI scientists had developed sophisticated geophysical equipment that helped "see into the ground." A brochure issued by SRI stated:

Archaeology—the recovery, restoration, and preservation of priceless artifacts from the past—is a classic science requiring years of training, experience, patience, and arduous adherence to time honored disciplines. In recent years SRI scientists with equipment capable of "seeing through" rock—cultural scientists trained in electronic sensing, geophysical methods, and remote sensing—have begun successfully to apply these recent technologies to expedite the important work of the archaeologist, anthropologist and historian. Remote sensing now offers an opportunity—for the first time—to explore and unearth some of man's great "lost" historic sites. Egypt and Israel offer particularly important opportunities.

The SRI equipment included a wall radar, seismic sounder, and cart mounted radar. If properly applied, this sophisticated equipment could most likely help solve the mystery of the location of the Temple.

Expedition Planned

On a trip to Israel in 1982, Don Stewart became involved with Lambert Dolphin and his SRI group. He also spent considerable time with Israelies who were interested in determining the location of the Temple. Don Stewart was invited to join an SRI expedition if and when it ever came about. One of the Israelis had assured us that the Moslem Waqf would cooperate with what we were intending to do. We just had to keep a low profile.

Goodman Incident

Plans were made to go to Israel in 1982 but were halted by the shooting on the Mount by Israeli soldier Allan Goodman. The trip was postponed to let tensions settle down. What appeared to be a good opportunity was now postponed and possibly cancelled.

Another Trip Planned

After letting the tensions cease for a while another tripped was planned in April/May of 1983. As we were about to leave we received the following Western Union Mailgram from Israel on April 8, 1983.

> Necessary authorities oppose project this time owing to adverse press.
> Regretfully must recommend postponement.
> Theo

Although this Israeli contact suggested we postpone again, we decided the trip should go ahead. In April-May of 1983 a seven man team headed by Lambert Dolphin, and including Don Stewart, made a six week geophysical survey in Israel. The group made use of SRI's highly sophisticated equipment including; cart radar, wall radar, seismic sounder, and high resolution resistivity. This non-destructive equipment was used on various archaeological sights in an attempt to determine what lay beneath the surface.

Our goal was to use the equipment as near as we could to the Temple Mount. However, before attempting that delicate task we decided to try out this sophisticated hardware on other sites. Working with several noted Israeli archaeologists we applied the equipment to a number of places around the country. Happily, the equipment worked very well causing one archaeologist to exclaim,"It works like magic." Assuredly there was no magic involved merely the careful skillful application of radar and sonar waves among the ancient ruins of Israel. The instruments showed the archaeologists some very promising possibilities as to where to excavate.

The Rabbinical Tunnel

Since 1967 an excavation sponsored by the Ministry of Religious Affairs has been going on near the prayer area of the Western Wall of the Temple Mount. This work has achieved little notoriety. The project consists of a tunnel running some 900 feet, running north alongside the Western Wall. The tunnel cuts its way beneath shops and houses in the Arab section of the Old City of Jerusalem. This site, hidden from public view, is known as the Rabbinical Tunnel.

In 1983 the tunnel was not accessible to the general public. We have both had the privilege to explore this magnificent site. It is a tremendous experience.

After entering from a locked metal door you start the journey some 60 feet above the bedrock at the hall under Wilson's Arch. However as you walk this level tunnel, the bedrock rises. When you reach the northern end of the tunnel you are about thirty feet *below* the bedrock's upper surface. The damp tunnel has a well lit corridor that is approximately seven feet high and five feet wide. One walks upon wooden floorboards.

There is one particularly amazing sight that steals your attention soon after you enter. It is a gigantic stone that is 46 feet long, over 10 feet high and about 10 feet deep. It is one solid piece of hewn limestone weighing over 415 tons! How the ancient builders brought that huge stone one half miles from the quarry is not known. It is also unknown how they were able to place the stones so precisely in the wall that a knife blade cannot slip in between the seams of the stones. This huge stone was one of many fascinating sights in the Rabbinical Tunnel.

A walk through the tunnel tends to put a person in a reflective mood when one thinks about the history that took place in and around these walls.

Since we could not operate with our equipment from the Temple Mount, our work would have to be carried out from this tunnel.

A Scientific Expedition is Thwarted

On May 22, 1983 our team of eight people including our affable Jewish guide, Eleazar, attempted to make the first scientific survey of the rabbinical tunnel. The object was to use our highly sophisticated equipment, including wall penetrating radar and seismic sounding, to look into the wall toward the Temple Mount in hopes of determining at least four things:

1) The thickness of the wall.

2) Any large open spaces inside the wall which could indicate a water cistern, a tunnel or a secret room.

3) The foundations of the Western Wall of the Second Temple or other structures. (The foundation stones may still be in place. Jesus predicted one stone would not be left upon another, but this may not include the foundation stone that is resting upon the bedrock).

4) Anything that had not been discovered thus far.

We went by night for two reasons. First we needed the quiet so that the instruments, especially the seismic sounder, could work at its best capacity, without interference of city noises and the workmen in the tunnel. Second, we thought it best to keep our mission quiet because the more people who knew about it the more complicated things became.

We arrived at the compound of the Western Wall at 10 p.m. The guard at the gate was about to let our van proceed when we were suddenly met by plain clothes detectives. They inquired as to what we were going to do. We told them who we were and that we had been invited by Rabbi Getz, the man in charge of the tunnel to do some scientific work for him. After examining our passports they called in their boss. After talking to us for a while he said that we could not come in because we did not have the proper permits. We were instructed to see a certain high official the next day who could grant us the proper permission. Thus we went back to the hotel, with a van full of unloaded equipment determined to get the proper permit first thing the next morning.

Afraid of a Riot

However a meeting with the chief of police intelligence early the next morning revealed that we needed no permit whatsoever. We were duly informed that the government police knew everything about us, who we were, why we were coming, and that they were placed at the compound to stop us.

The reason for this was they had received a call from the Waqf (the Moslem high command) that went as follows: "some scientists from America are going to place electronic equipment underneath our Mosque, please stop them."

The chief detective said that we had done nothing wrong and that which we were trying to do was a legal and a worthy venture. However, they feared what the Moslems might do if we were allowed to continue. Therefore, to avoid a possible riot and international incident (as had occurred with the ill-fated Parker expedition), we were refused permission to enter. They were sympathetic to our effort, going out of their way to make sure we were not offended. They told us that it was their hope that we could, sometime soon, return and perform our desired task.

However, since the Moslems do not understand our equipment they most likely assume it to be something destructive rather than constructive.

The conclusion of the whole episode is as follows: Even though the rabbinical tunnel is on Jewish property and we had a request by those who have charge of it to perform a legitimate scientific study, we could not do it because of Moslem objections. Thus, the Moslems seemingly have veto power over what goes on in the tunnel as well as on the Temple Mount. The authorities, wanting to keep the status quo, bent to the Moslem wishes in hopes to avoid possible confrontation. Needless to say, the situation remains highly volatile.

Naturally we were disappointed that we could not perform the purpose of our trip to Israel. Though we were foiled in our attempt to use the equipment on or near the Temple Mount we are confident that if we were given the chance again, the team could accomplish something significant. We know that the equipment can and does work in the terrain of Israel.

Expedition Receives Notoriety

Though we did not achieve our desired goal our expedition did attract attention. The Jerusalem *Post* ran the following story:

> Arming archeologists with electronic devices to probe the ground would seem to take the sporting element out of the exercise—like providing bullfighters with RPG's.
>
> But Israeli archeologists, like their colleagues abroad, have been quick to place science above sport when offered the opportunity of abetting their instincts with electronics.
>
> Some of the most sophisticated equipment in the world for taking soundings through the ground and thick walls was recently employed on several of the most notable digs in the country by an American group that developed its expertise in defence work for the U.S. government.
>
> The group, headed by physicist Lambert Dolphin, is part of SRI International of Menlo Park, California . . . They brought with them equipment that included ground-penetrating radar and electrodes employed in a "high resolution automatic resistivity" method said to be capable of drawing an underground contour map. . .
>
> In Hebron, the team took readings of the ground beneath the Tomb of the Patriarchs while remaining outside the structure. However, the planned highlight of the visit—a probe of the Temple Mount—did not come off.
>
> Dolphin said he had received permission from the rabbi of the Western Wall, Rabbi Yehuda Getz, to position his equipment in the tunnel dug by the Religious Affairs Ministry north of the Western Wall. His intention was to probe electronically beneath the mount to see whether he could find indications of subterranean passages in which objects of historical or religious significance may have been buried.
>
> However, as the team approached the tunnel they were intercepted and turned back by Israeli police operating at the behest of the Supreme Moslem Council, which had apparently been warned of their activities by Moslem officials in Hebron.[1]

The trip also received publicity in the United States. The Sacramento Bee ran the following story:

IMAGINE INDIANA JONES WITH HAN SOLO GADGETRY

The tomb lay buried—secreted under a fall of rock from another burial site.

For centuries, grave robbers passed it by. Archeologists, armed with educated guesses, fumbled blindly around it.

It took British archeologist Howard Carter six years of searching through hot dust and rocks before in 1922, he uncovered the tomb of Tutankhamen, boy king of Egypt. It had stayed untouched, crammed with the trappings of a king, for more than 3,000 years.

Recently a group of California engineers retraced Carter's tracks. Standing as he did in a dark tomb above Tutankhamen's, they set up acoustic sound equipment.

It took them thirty minutes to get a reading on the burial site beneath their feet. "That's what we can do best-save time," says Lambert Dolphin, a physicist with SRI International, a private research firm in Menlo Park. Dolphin was one member of the team that "rediscovered" Tut's tomb. . .

As well as working in Egypt, the SRI team has helped sort through buried cities in Israel. Last year, it discovered a chamber inside what was thought to be a solid tower in the mountain fortress of Herodium, the summer residence of Herod the Great. Israeli archeologists excavating the site think the chamber—15 feet in diameter—could be the tomb of Herod, who ruled from 73 B.C. to 4 A.D. Archeologists have been searching for the tomb, thought to be full of gold and artwork for years.

"We've given some hot leads in a needle-in-a-haystack search" Dolphin said. But now they still have to do the excavation and that takes time. I want to make the point that archeology is a time-honored profession and while this equipment can help, it will never replace the plain old hard work.[2]

Because the team had possibly discovered Herod's tomb the wire services picked up the story and it became printed nation wide. Some of the Headlines read as follows:

Physicist Says He Has Found Herod's Tomb,
The New Haven Connecticut Register, October 30, 1983

Geophysicist Looks For Herod's Tomb With Aid Of Radar, Sonar *Times Union,* Albany, N.Y., November 24, 1983

The SRI team *never* claimed to have found Herod's tomb, only a possible site. However some of the newspapers did sensationalize the story making our expedition seemingly the discoverers of Herod's burial place. While this may be the case, any announcements ahead of time are premature.

Ehud Netzer, the excavator of Herodium, does not believe Herod was buried in the chamber in the tower which we discovered. Only time will tell whether Herod's burial place has been discovered by SRI's highly sophisticated equipment.

However what we the expedition did prove is that the equipment works. The tower in which the chamber was discovered was always thought to be solid. No one would have ever bothered attempting to excavate it if it were not for the wall penetrating radar. The work at Herodium proved again what a valuable service these instruments can render. If applied to the Temple Mount the same results can be obtained.

More Controversy

An article that appeared in the Jerusalem Post further fueled the controversy:

> There are significant, and to some minds worrisome links between a handful of American Evangelical leaders and right-wing Israelis like [Stanley] Goldfoot. Some of the personalities on his board are important men. Lambert Dolphin, heads a key section of the world's most massive research conglomerate, the Stanford Research Institute, a $200-million-a-year concern whose main clients are the U.S. government and corporations like Bechtel . . .
>
> Before the Temple Mount plotters—both the Lifta terrorists and the Gush Emunim terror group— were arrested, Goldfoot and Dolphin planned to hover one day just before dawn in a helicopter 300 metres above the Temple Mount and the Holy of Holies (where the Ark of the Covenant was kept), and to X-ray and probe the innards of the mount with Dolphin's induced polarization set, Cesium Beam Magnatometer, downhole Borescope television and high-power Dipole-Dipole Resistivity Set to find out just what is buried down there . . . Along with Lambert Dolphin they [Other Christian Temple Mount Activists] condemned the abortive attempt (by the Lifta Group) to blow up the Dome of the Rock. But they feel "violence" is being done to the most sacred site

"when Jewish prayer books are seized by Temple Guards from devout Jewish women.[3]

Because of the numerous inaccuracies in the article Lambert Dolphin immediately sent a letter to the Jerusalem *Post.* It reads in part:

Your article . . . contains so many distortions of fact and so much vilification directed at well intentioned Israelis and friends of friends of Israel I can not help but wonder if this is part of a conspiracy of some kind? I deeply regret the cheap attacks on my good friend Stanley Goldfoot who has spent much time and taken much trouble to free me from anti-Semitism and ignorance of Jewish values and Jewish consciousness.

The latter trip [to Israel] when I was accompanied by six colleagues consisted of donated geophysical services to half a dozen leading Israeli archaeologists intended to advance the state of Archaeological knowledge and methodology in Israel. This work was paid for by four American Christians and one Jewish businessman. All funds were used for team expenses and salaries. No funds were donated or passed to any individual or group in Israel. I regret not having additional funds, as I would be glad to contribute them to your nation's leading archaeologists to be used at their discretion for their important excavation work.

I would like to see the Temple rebuilt, but am not a member of the Jerusalem Temple Foundation nor do I wish to participate in the building planning or program. This effort, I believe, is part of the Jewish religious economy, not the calling of God for the church. Of course I would like to see the Temple Mount explored scientifically and non-destructively apart from all religious and political considerations. I believe freedom of worship and prayer on the Temple Mount should now be extended to include Jews and Christians and that by faith the Jewish people should regain administration of the Temple Mount as part of your own legitimate religious and Biblical heritage given you by God. I deplore the widespread apathy, indifference and hostility toward the holy one in the holy land knowing this only speeds the "time of Jacob's trouble" which will be marked by terrible trial and much suffering as the prophets have all said. Israel's glorious destiny is sure and for that I rejoice. You seem to not need any external enemies since there is so much in-country backbiting, character assassination and self-destructiveness. Friends you do need, and I remain a friend and supporter of the people and state of

Israel in spite of being misunderstood and misrepresented.[4]

Other Methods

As of today, no one knows for certain which of the possible sites on the Temple Mount was the place where the First and Second Temple stood. If our team had been permitted to use the sophisticated equipment in the Rabbinical Tunnel, then we have reason to believe that we may have been able to help solve the problem. There are, however, other scientific methods that could be used to settle the issue.

The Rabbinical Arches

It was required that sacred structures not be placed upon burial sites. The texts which pertain to the construction of holy sites prohibit the building upon a grave site or over dead bones. Even if a proposed building site was on bedrock, the rabbis were concerned that there could, in theory, at least, still be dead bones deeper down. Since one could never be certain that there were not burial grounds below a sacred structure, rabbinical practice involved a form of multiple archways to isolate the structure from any possibilities of desecration from burials below the intended structure. An initial series of arches were then followed by a second series, offset from the first, similar to the manner of common bricklaying. The rationale was that this would isolate the final structure from contact with any subterranean grave site. The resulting voids which one would expect under the Temple Mount offer an opportunity for detection by sonic or other means. Preliminary probes by ground penetrating radar do indicate that there are voids under the southern portion of the Temple Mount, giving tentative encouragement to those who favor this view.

THE NEXT STEPS: WHAT ELSE CAN BE DONE?

There are a number of advanced technologies which are non-invasive and which could yield valuable insights as to what lies below the present surface of the Temple Mount.

Aerial Photography

Systematic aerial photography, conducted on a seasonal basis, is likely to yield many insights. It is remarkable what current techniques can reveal. These techniques have proven fruitful at Stonehenge on the Salisbury Plain in England, and elsewhere.[5]

Infra-Red (Thermographic) Recording

Infra-red techniques are suitable for mapping subtle surface temperature differences which, in turn, can yield insights into the underlying structures. The infra-red portion of the frequency spectrum is widely used by the military and these techniques are also beneficial in industrial and medical applications.

Differences in heat emission can reveal much of what is going on below a surface. By scanning the Temple Mount from the air, the thermal gradients are very likely to reveal subterranean structures, voids and the like. Such structures can include cisterns, drainage tunnels, subterranean chambers and other discontinuities. The most effective approach would be to record multiple frequency bands simultaneously during a number of flights at different times and seasons. Such a program should yield major insights concerning the location of the original Temples.

Ground Penetrating Radar

As mentioned earlier, it has proven feasible for radar to penetrate the ground to a distance of 10 - 15 meters, under the right conditions. The authors had the opportunity to participate with Lambert Dolphin and his SRI group in originally introducing these techniques to the archaeological community in Israel in 1983 and these techniques have been continued by local Israelis.

Recent probes suggest that there are, indeed, voids below the floor level of the Hulda Gate in the sections south of the Dome of the Rock. These are suggestive of open archways which are in accordance with rabbinical practice.

Systematic use of this technology is likely to be one of the most fruitful technologies over the near term.

Magnetic Anomaly Detection

The sensing of disturbances and discontinuities in the earth's magnetic field has proven effective in detecting magnetic and conducting (metallic) elements below the surface of the earth or the oceans. One example of the exploitation of these techniques is their use in anti-submarine warfare where it is possible, under certain circumstances, to detect a submarine from a properly equipped aircraft. "Magnetic Anomaly Detection, ("MAD" gear) was widely used in World War II.

Since the Ark of the Covenant was covered with gold, it would be highly conductive and, if it is, indeed, hidden under the Temple Mount, it might yield to this type of search technology.

Resistivity Studies

It is possible to precisely measure the resistivity of the ground between two points on the surface. By carefully arranging a grid of such measurements, an underground contour map could be compiled and indications of the underlying structure can sometimes be gained. These techniques are very subtle and are best used in concert with other techniques for corroboration.

Remote Seismic Sensors

The exploitation of seismic (200 - 400 Hz) sensors may also prove useful in understanding the subterranean structures underlying the Temple Mount. Like most of the more exotic techniques, they are most likely to prove fruitful when used in concert with other forms of instrumentation.

Microgravity Sensors

While very difficult to apply in practice, highly sensitive measurements of changes in gravity can yield insights when large masses or discontinuities are involved.

Radioactive Isotopes

It has been proposed that by placing radioactive isotopes in the ground water, and then tracing the flow of subterranean streams, some clues as to the underlying structures might be gained.

Acoustic Holography

By precise time-phased recording of the response to acoustical impulses, it is possible to use a computer to construct a synthetic hologram of the underlying structure.[6] A hologram is a fourier transform of a spatial image and can be a profoundly useful three-dimensional image of the space of interest.

If permission could be obtained, an appropriate grid of acoustic sensors, perhaps interconnected by fibre optic cables, could be arranged on the Temple Mount. With the appropriate acoustic illumination, perhaps by a remote pile driver, a computer synthesis of the resultant recordings should yield a three-dimensional "map" of the structures below the present surface.

The establishment of a proper sensor grid would require permission and access to the Temple Mount. Under the present regime, such permission appears unlikely.

Technology Conferences Planned

As with all of these advanced techniques, they simply await the necessary resources and commitment. There are frequent periodic meetings among the various parties interested in the Temple Mount, and there appears to be a cooperative spirit among them, despite their different viewpoints, about the location of the Temple.

The authors have been invited to participate in a series of technology conferences on the Temple Mount and there are many reasons to be optimistic that the next few years will yield some remarkable insights and resolve many of the scholastic and scientific controversies.

Summary

The present situation is that the instruments of modern science, for political reasons, have not been able to be applied to the Temple Mount. It is clear that the major issues will be political, not scientific. They will be resolved by leadership, not technology. A highly persuasive, charismatic leader will emerge on the horizon who may be the key to resolving these issues.

Endnotes

1. Abraham Rabinovich, Jerusalem *Post,* August 1, 1983.

2. Deborah Blum, Sacramento *Bee,* Sunday, October 14, 1984.

3. Louis Rapoport, "Slouching Toward Armageddon: Links with Evangelicals," Jerusalem *Post,* June 1984.

4. Lambert Dolphin, Letter to the Jerusalem *Post,* July 6, 1984.

5. Gerald S. Hawkins, *Stonehenge Decoded,* Dell Publishing Co., New York, 1965.

6. Dr Alex Metherell, Acoustical Holography, Scientific American, October, 1969. Dr. Metherell is a close associate of the authors, and first proposed such a project for the Temple Mount in 1980.

CHAPTER TWELVE

THE COMING TEMPLE: CENTER STAGE FOR THE FINAL COUNTDOWN

And the people of the prince that shall come shall destroy
the city and the sanctuary; and the end thereof shall be
with a flood, . . . And he shall confirm the covenant with
many for one week: and in the midst of the week he shall
cause the sacrifice and the oblation to cease, and for the
overspreading of abominations he shall make it desolate.

Daniel 9:26,27

Why Are We So Certain?

How can we be so sure that the Temple will really be
rebuilt? Because the Bible says so. Numerous passages in
the Old Testament,[1] and at least three passages in the
New Testament,[2] make it clear that the Temple will be
rebuilt in Jerusalem.[3]

The preparations for the literal fulfillment of these
Biblical prophecies make this period one of the most
exciting times in human history. In the coming years, we
are about to witness the climax of God's plan for mankind!

Unresolved Matters

Given the state of the situation as it now stands there
are two important matters that are still unresolved.

The first issue concerns the location of the Third
Temple. Before a Third Temple can be constructed the
exact location must be determined. Did the Temple
originally stand at the present site of the Dome of the
Rock? Is the theory by Dr. Asher Kaufman that the Temple
was located approximately 100 meters to the north of the
Dome correct? How about others who have suggested that
the Temple was located elsewhere on the Mount such as
between the Dome of the Rock and the Al Aqsa Mosque?

Before the Third Temple can be built the location must be clearly determined.

HOW ARE THEY GOING TO BUILD IT?

The second problem, assuming they know the correct site, is how are they going to build it? How could the Jews construct a Third Temple upon the site of a sacred spot of Islam? There have been, at least, six proposed solutions:

1. Tear Down the Dome

When Israel became a state in 1948, Rabbi Levy of the Tremount Temple of New York said: "The Temple of Jerusalem will be rebuilt . . . It is more than possible that the very religious will insist on tearing down the Mosque and erecting a Temple much like Solomon's."

As we have already noted, the leader of the Temple Mount Faithful, Gershon Salomon, has said, "I'm sorry but the Mosque must be moved."

The mind boggles at what would happen if the Jews undertook to demolish the Dome of the Rock and replace it with a Temple. Destroying sacred Moslem buildings upon the Temple Mount would be an invitation for the destruction of Israel. It is unthinkable that the government of Israel would allow anything like this.

2. Purchase the Temple Mount

There is also the possibility that the Dome of the Rock could be bought. Shortly after the Six Day War in 1967, a letter came to the Moslem Council in Jerusalem from a substantial Jewish organization in the United States offering to buy the Temple Mount, with the Al Aqsa Mosque and the Dome of the Rock. The price offered was 100 million dollars. The Moslems told them it was not for sale.

3. Natural Disaster

A third suggestion is that some natural disaster will occur that will destroy the Dome of the Rock. This could be an earthquake, explosion or some other natural disaster. It has also been suggested that an errant missile may destroy the Dome.

The obvious problem with this view, is that the Moslem world would immediately want it rebuilt if it were destroyed either accidentally or on purpose.

4. Joint Project

Others have suggested a joint project, with Moslems and Jews working together on the Temple Mount. They would put aside their differences and build a Third Temple together, as a monument to peace. Aryeh Kotzer, principal of a school of religion in Israel, has published a booklet in which he maintains that the Dome of the Rock could simply be incorporated into the Third Temple. In light of history, this suggestion seems impossible but stranger things have been known to happen.

5. Different Site in Jerusalem

Some have suggested that the Temple be built on a different site in the city of Jerusalem. There are many who believe the Great Synagogue, next door to Solomon's palace in Jerusalem, will be the site of the Third Temple. However, Solomon's palace (Hechel Slomo) is not a palace at all. It is, rather, the headquarters of the chief Rabbi's of Israel. It has nothing to do with the Temple. It was not named after King Solomon of the Bible, but after Slomo (Solomon) Wolfson whose family contributed toward its building.

No other site will suffice for the Temple. The Bible commands that the Temple be built upon the site that God chose:

> But you shall seek the place where the Lord your God chooses, out of all your tribes put His name for His habitation; and there you shall go . . . but in the place the Lord chooses, in one of your tribes, there you shall offer your burnt offerings, and there you shall do all that I commanded you (Deuteronomy 12:5,14).

6. Built Elsewhere Upon the Mount

A final possibility is that the Temple could be built elsewhere on the Mount. We have considered two alternative theories as to the location of the Temple. If either proves to be correct, then a Third Temple could be built without removing either the Dome of the Rock or the Al Aqsa Mosque. It would also solve the age-old question as to how the Temple could be built upon the Mount without causing a "holy war." If the Dome of the Rock does not have to be removed then theoretically a Third Temple could be built adjacent to it.

Revelation 11

What makes the Kaufman hypothesis so provocative is, that if Dr. Kaufman is correct, the Temple apparently could conceivably be built without disturbing the Dome of the Rock. The Dome of the Rock would be presently sitting in what was the Outer Court of the Temple.

Many have speculated that perhaps the Temple could be rebuilt without disturbing the Dome of the Rock, leaving the Outer Court undedicated.

If that turns out to be the case, it would conform precisely to a vision given to the Apostle John in the Book of Revelation. John, apparently transported forward through time, is given a vision of the Temple Mount.

> Then I was given a reed like a measuring rod. And the angel stood, saying, "Rise and measure the temple of God, the altar and those who worship there. But leave out the court which is outside the temple, and do not measure it, for it has been given to the Gentiles. And they will tread the holy city under foot for forty-two months (Revelation 11:1,2).

The word for Temple is ναος (naos) that is, the temple proper, exclusive of the courts. The reference to the Outer Court—the Court of the Gentiles—is strange in that it should be singled out. This is highly suggestive that the Temple may be built without disturbing the Dome of the Rock. This has given the Kaufman hypothesis substantial popularity among some of the Christian community.

This could also be true for the southern hypothesis, but it is harder to imagine the Temple satisfactorily sandwiched between the Dome of the Rock and Al Aqsa Mosque. But then, who knows? We'll just wait and see.

How Could This Be?

There are many who deny this possibility. Since the Moslems consider the entire Temple Mount as a mosque it is unlikely that they would allow a Third Temple to be built on their holy ground. To them it would be an abomination, an affront to Allah. A Temple, side by side to the Dome of the Rock would be impossible to conceive. In addition,

Moslem theology claims that land once owned by Islam is forever holy to Islam and must be repossessed if lost. This makes the Temple Mount theirs forever.

Furthermore many Jews scoff at the idea of a Temple built in the backyard of the Dome of the Rock. What kind of glorious Temple would this be, they ask? They believe that it would be an outrage architecturally, aesthetically and historically. With both Moslems and Jews opposed to this idea, it would take a diplomatic miracle to allow these holy sites to stand next to each other. Who could pull off such a coup?

The Coming World Leader

The Bible indicates that there will emerge on the international scene a leader, the likes of which the world has never seen. He will be the most persuasive, charismatic problem-solver to ever make the front pages. He will establish a program for peace that will cause the entire world to look to him for leadership. He will appear to be the ultimate answer for this troubled world of ours.

Among his many exploits, he will be accepted by Israel as their Messiah! He apparently will be instrumental in facilitating the rebuilding of the Temple and re-establishing the Temple worship.

The Authors' Burden

It is with mixed feelings that we observe the global circumstances setting the stage for the emergence of this remarkable leader.

On the one hand, we can't help but feel excited as we observe the ancient scenarios predicted in the Bible begin to actually happen in our time:

Surely the Lord God does nothing, unless He reveals His secret unto His servants the prophets (Amos 3:7).

On the other hand, it is with the pain akin to that of Jeremiah that we realize that this coming leader, although he will be embraced as Israel's Messiah, he will betray them and usher in a time of trouble yet unequalled in human history.

The Betrayal

A complete description of the origin, career, and destiny of this remarkable leader is far beyond the scope of this brief review of the Temple.[4] But a few highlights are essential to properly focus the rebuilding of the Temple and his role with respect to it.

The prophet Daniel was given a remarkable prophecy by the angel Gabriel which is recorded in Daniel 9.[5] The climax of this amazing passage is a final "week" of years (the "Seventieth Week" in Biblical parlance) which is defined by a treaty involving Israel and confirmed by this world leader.

However, in the middle of this period—after 3 1/2 years—he will renege on his commitments and "cause the sacrifice and oblation to cease."[6] He will betray Israel, set himself up to be worshipped, and usher in a time of persecution "such as the world had never seen to that time, nor would ever see again." Jesus said, "Unless those days be shortened, there would no flesh be saved."

This leader's desecration of the Temple has a technical name: "The abomination of desolation." In fact, Jesus, in His private prophetic briefing to His disciples, indicated that this unique act would be the key event at the time of the end:

> Therefore when you see the 'abomination of desolation, spoken of by Daniel the prophet, standing in the holy place (let the reader understand), then let those who are in Judea flee to the mountains. Let him who is on the housetop not come down to take anything out of his house. And let him who is in the field not turn back to get his clothes. But woe to those who are pregnant and to those with nursing babies in those days! And pray that your flight may not be in winter, or on a Sabbath. For then there will be great tribulation, such as has not occurred since the beginning of the world until this time, no, nor ever shall. And unless those days were shortened, no flesh would be saved; but for elect's sake those days will be shortened (Matthew 24:15-22).

Note the references "to those who are in Judea" and the "sabbath day:" this passage is directed to the Jews, not Gentiles.

The Abomination of Desolation

Fortunately, we have a historical precedent to better understand this strange phrase, "the abomination of desolation."

The desecration of the Second Temple by Antiochus Epiphanes (p. 44) in 167 B.C. involved the enforcement of false worship and the desecration of the Holy of Holies. This event was in the past when Jesus briefed His disciples; His reference was toward the future.

The "abomination of desolation" is the central event in the "Seventieth Week" of Daniel's famous prophecy.[7] It is still yet to happen.

The Man of Sin, The Son of Perdition

This coming world leader will be received by Israel as their Messiah. Jesus said,

> I have come in My Father's name, and you do not receive Me; if another comes in his own name, him you will receive (John 5:43).

The Apostle Paul adds an additional insight:

> Let no one deceive you by any means; for that Day will not come unless the falling away comes first, and the man of sin is revealed, the son of perdition, who opposes and exalts himself above all that is called God or that is worshiped, so that he sits as God in the temple of God, showing himself that he is God (2 Thessalonians 2:3,4).

Bible Commentator R. C. H. Lenski notes:

> The sense is plain to the ordinary reader whether he be Greek or English. This Antichrist reveals himself as the Antichrist by this pagan act of seating himself in the true God's own sanctuary . . . he does it by this pagan act, the climax of all anti-Christianity. He sits in God's own place as if he, too, were God and shows and exhibits himself to all Christendom with the claim "that he is God," that no less than deity belongs also to him. This very idea of extending deity in this way is utterly pagan. The great apostasy accepts this claim and honors this Antichrist with divine honor. That is what constitutes this apostasy. When Paul wrote, the people of God had never seen an apostasy and an Antichrist like this; nor has there been another who is comparable to this one since that time.[8]

There is a widespread tendency in Christian circles to refer to this coming leader as the "Antichrist." Of the dozens of labels that the Bible uses for him, that particular term can be myopic and misleading.

Note that this person "exalts himself above all that is called God." Doesn't that include "Allah"? Will he somehow, be able to gain homage from both Moslems and Jews?

The Antichrist

The term Antichrist is made up of two Greek words *anti* which means "in the place of," or "instead of," and *Christ* which is the "anointed one" or "Messiah." Thus the Antichrist is a person who attempts to take the rightful place of the true Messiah.

The Scripture defines Antichrist in the following manner:

> Who is a liar but he who denies that Jesus is the Christ? He is antichrist who denies the Father and the Son (1 John 2:22).

Many Antichrists

The Bible teaches that many antichrists will arise throughout the course of the present age.

> And Jesus answered and said to them: "Take heed that no one deceives you. For many will come in My name, saying, 'I am the Christ,' and will deceive many . . .
> Then many false prophets will rise up and deceive many . . .
> Then if anyone says to you, 'Look, here is the Christ!' or 'There!' do not believe it. For false Christs and false prophets will arise and show great signs and wonders, so as to deceive if possible, even the elect. See I have told you beforehand. Therefore if they say to you, 'Look He is in the desert!' do not go out; or 'Look, He is in the inner rooms!' do not believe it. For as the lightning flashes from the east to the west, so also will the coming of the Son of Man be" (Matthew 24:4,5,11,23-27).

> Little children, it is the last hour; and as you have heard that the Antichrist is coming, even now many antichrists have come, by which we know that it is the last hour . . . and every spirit that does not confess that Jesus Christ is come in the flesh is not of God. And this is

the spirit of the Antichrist, which you have heard was coming, and is now already in the world . . . For many deceivers have gone out into the world who do not confess Jesus Christ as coming in the flesh. This is a deceiver and an antichrist (1 John 2:18,4:3; 2 John 7).

False Messiah

Throughout the history of the church there have been those who claimed to be the Christ. These false christs well fit the Scripture that tells us many antichrists shall come. History has already recorded a number of people who have claimed to be Christ and have gathered disciples. False christs will continue to appear until He comes again.

The Final Antichrist

Although many antichrists will arise during the true church age, the Bible speaks of a future Antichrist who will come on the scene before the Second Coming of Christ.

The Dictionary of the Bible describes the Antichrist in the following manner:

The great opponent and counterpart of the true Messiah, by whom he is finally to be conquered . . . the idea was present in Judaism and developed with the growth of the Messianic hope. . . while the precise term Antichrist is lacking in Jewish literature, the idea of an opponent who persecutes God's people and is ultimately to be conquered by the Messiah is an integral part of the general hope born in prophetism . . . [The] idea may fairly be said to have been in Daniel 11:26 . . . Also Zechariah 12:14.9

The Rise of Antichrist

The Antichrist will rise to power, not as a religious leader but as a political leader. He will head up a ten nation political confederation that will be a revival of the old Roman Empire. He produces unity among this group while establishing himself as a strong political ruler. As the head of this confederation, he makes a covenant with the nation Israel, which gives the world the impression that he is a man of peace. The prophet Daniel wrote:

And in his place shall arise a vile person, to whom they will not give the honor of royalty; but he shall come in peaceably, and seize the kingdom by intrigue. With the force of a flood they shall be swept away from before him and be broken, and also the prince of the covenant. And after a league is made with him he shall act deceitfully, for he shall come up and become strong with a small number of people. He shall enter peaceably, even unto the riches places of the province; and he shall do what his fathers have not done, nor his forefathers: he shall disperse among them the plunder, spoil, and riches; and he shall devise his plans against the strongholds, but only for a time (Daniel 11:21-24).

The Bible says that one of the things that will characterize the environment in the last days is a false peace:

For when they say, 'Peace and safety!' then sudden destruction comes on them, as labor pains on a pregnant woman. And they shall not escape (1 Thessalonians 5:3).

Though he appears to be a man of peace, he is actually a man of deceit energized by Satan, to lead astray the people of the earth.

World Dictator

Eventually the Antichrist becomes the world dictator who will exercise control over the people of the earth:

So they worshipped the dragon which gave authority to the beast; and they worshipped the beast, saying, "Who is like the beast? Who is able to make war with him? (Revelation 13:4).

He then takes over the Temple in Jerusalem claiming to be the long-awaited Messiah. The Antichrist also claims to be God.[10]

Life to His Image

The Antichrist's cohort, the false prophet, then gives life to an image of the beast causing the inhabitants of the earth to worship the beast and his image:

Then I saw another beast coming up out of the earth, and he had two horns like a lamb and spoke like a dragon. And he exercises all the authority of the first beast in his presence, and causes the earth and those who dwell in it to worship the first beast, whose deadly wound was healed. He performs great signs, so that he even makes fire come down from heaven on the earth in the sight of men. And he deceives those who dwell on the earth by those signs, which he was granted to do in the sight of the beast, telling those who dwell on the earth to make an image to the beast who was wounded by the sword and lived. He was granted power to give breath to the image of the beast, that the image of the beast should both speak and cause as many as would not worship the image of the beast to be killed (Revelation 13:11-15).

The Antichrist will apparently pull off a counterfeit resurrection in his diabolical plan to divert the people from the true Messiah.

Persecuting God's People

The Antichrist will then turn on both the Jews and the believers in Jesus, persecuting them and speaking blasphemies against God:

Then he opened his mouth in blasphemy against God, to blaspheme His name, His tabernacle, and those who dwell in heaven. And it was granted to him to make war with the saints and overcome them. And authority was given him over every tribe, tongue, and nation (Revelation 13:6,7).

Then the King shall do according to his own will: he shall exalt and magnify himself above every god, shall speak blasphemies against the God of gods, and shall prosper till the wrath has been accomplished; for what has been determined shall be done. He shall regard neither the God of his fathers nor the desire of women, nor regard any god; for he shall magnify himself above them all (Daniel 11:36-38).

The Great Tribulation

The Great Tribulation is a time of God's judgment of the people of the earth:

For there will be great tribulation, such as has not been since the beginning of the world until this time, no, nor ever shall be (Matthew 24:21) .

Jesus was referring to the Book of Daniel when He used this language:

At that time Michael shall stand up, the great prince who stands watch over the sons of your people; and there shall be a time of trouble, such as never was since there was a nation, even to that time (Daniel 12:1,2).

Jesus said that the terrible judgments would be cut short for the sake of the survival of humanity.

And unless those days were shortened, no flesh would be saved; but for the elect's sake those days will be shortened (Matthew 24:22).

The seven year period is divided into two periods of three and one half years each. The first three and one half years will be a time of relative peace, where the people will be lulled by the Antichrist into the false notion that they are dwelling in safety.

At the midst of the seven year period, the Antichrist will break his promises to the Jews, and begin persecuting them and the believers in Jesus. It is during this three and one half year period that the great judgments occur and the Great Tribulation begins. The prophet Jeremiah spoke of this period as "the time of Jacob's trouble" (Jeremiah 30:7).

New Monetary System

There will also be a new monetary system set up by this man of sin:

And he causes all, both small and great, rich and poor, free and slave, to receive a mark on their right hand or on their foreheads, and that no one may buy or sell except one who has the mark or the name of the beast, or the number of his name. Here is wisdom. Let him who has understanding calculate the number of the beast, for it is the number of a man: His number is 666 (Revelation 13:16-18).

Over the centuries this famous number, 666, has given rise to many conjectures as to whom it refers. Many theories continue in our present day as to the potential identity of this person.

Second Coming of Christ

His plan to rule the world and destroy God's people is thwarted by the Second Coming of Christ:

And I saw the beast, the kings of the earth, and their armies, gathered together to make war against Him who sat on the horse and against His army. Then the beast was captured and with him the false prophet who worked signs in His presence, by which he deceived those who received the mark of the beast and those who worshiped his image. These two were cast alive into the lake of fire burning with brimstone. And the rest were killed with the sword which proceeded from the mouth of Him who sat on the horse. And all the birds were filled with their flesh . . . And the devil, who deceived them, was cast into the lake of fire and brimstone where the beast and the false prophet are. And they will be tormented day and night forever and ever (Revelation 19:19-21;20:10).

Thus we have the inglorious end of this false Messiah, his followers, and the godless system he installed.

When Christ returns it will be clear to everyone, for He will return visibly, personally and in judgment.

The Mount of Olives

When Jesus entered Jerusalem at His triumphal entry, He came from the Mount of Olives. Matthew records that He fulfilled a prophecy made by Zechariah (Zechariah 9:9).

Zechariah has made another prophecy concerning the Mount of Olives that has yet to be fulfilled:

And in that day His feet will stand on the Mount of Olives, which faces Jerusalem on the east. And the Mount of Olives shall be split in two, from east to west, making a very large valley; half of the mountain shall move toward the north and half of it toward the south (Zechariah 14:4).

Jesus ascended into heaven from the Mount of Olives. When He returns He will set His feet back upon the Mount. When Jesus returns the geography will be changed:

And in that day it shall be that living waters shall flow from Jerusalem, half of them toward the eastern sea and half of them toward the western sea; in both summer and winter it shall occur (Zechariah 14:8).

He then will set up His Kingdom, of which there will be no end. His assumption to the throne of David which was promised to Mary (Luke 1:32) will take place at this time. The prophecies concerning the Messiah will have been completely fulfilled.

Summary

The Temple Mount, which has figured so prominently in the plan of God for the past 4,000 years, has an inglorious future according to the Bible. It will be the scene of the event that triggers the beginning of the Great Tribulation upon the earth. The Jews, thinking they have their long-awaited Messiah, will actually be accepting the one that comes in place of God's anointed. This deceit will become obvious only after a time of pseudo-peace on the earth.

Jesus Christ will put an end to this terrible time when He returns to earth and sets us His eternal kingdom. He will eventually create a new heaven and a new earth where there will be no further need for a Temple.[11]

And I saw no Temple in it, for the Lord God, the Almighty, and the Lamb, are its Temple (Revelation 21:22,23).

The Lord God Himself will dwell with His people for all eternity. This is the glorious promise of Scripture.

Endnotes

1. Daniel 9:27, 11:31, and 12:11; (et al...).

2. Matthew 24:15, 2 Thessalonians 2:4, and Revelation 11:1,2.

Note on the Possible Role of Television:

    During our discussions at the Temple Institute, we were surprised to discover a planned electrical wiring diagram for the planned Temple. When we inquired about it, they explained that where the Tanach (the Old Testament), the Talmud, the Mishna, and other sacred sources prescribe specifics, they intend to the comply as faithfully as possible. But where the ancient sources are silent, they feel free to exploit advanced technologies. "After all, we are building a temple for the future, not the past."
    Jesus may have predicted television facilities. "When you therefore shall see the abomination of desolation. . . stand in the holy place . . . Then let them which be in Judea flee into the mountains. . ." How can those in Judea "see" something taking place in the Holy of Holies?

3. A brief summary of the reasons for this confidence has been included as Appendix 1.

4. A summary of Biblical references have been included as Appendix 6 for the diligent inquirer.

5. This passage includes one of the most remarkable prophecies in the Bible. A brief summary has been included as Appendix 4.

6. Daniel 9:27.

7. Chapters 6 through 19 of the book of Revelation is an expansion of this period, climaxing the "Day of the Lord."

8. R. C. H. Lenski, *The Interpretation of St. Paul's Epistles to the Colossians, the Thessalonians, to Timothy, to Titus and to Philemon,* Minneapolis, Minnesota, Augsburg Publishing House, 1937, pp. 411,412.

9. James Hastings, Editor, The Dictionary of the Bible, Scribner, 1963. p. 208.

10. Dr. F.F Bruce observes: ἐπὶ πάντα λεγόμενον θεὸν ἢ σέβασμα, "over every so called God or object of worship." The addition of λεγόμενον before θεὸν implies that the man of lawlessness elevates himself above the living and true God and every other so-called God. The more comprehensive σέβασμα denotes (as in Acts 17:23) any object of worship. The language echoes that in which Antiochus IV is depicted in Dan. 11:26,37: Antiochus the willful king, is to "exalt himself and magnify himself above every god" (ἐπὶ πάντα θεὸν).
F.F. Bruce, Word Bible Commentary, 1 & 2 Thessalonians, Waco Texas, Word, 1982, p. 168.

11. See our discussion in Appendix 5.

CHAPTER THIRTEEN

WHAT DOES IT ALL MEAN?

Now it shall come to pass in the latter days that the mountain of the Lord's house shall be established on the top of the moutains, and shall be exalted above the hills; and all the nations shall flow to it. Many people shall come and say, "Come let us go up to the mountain of the Lord, to the house of the God of Jacob; He will teach us His ways, and we shall walk in His paths. For out of Zion shall go forth the law, and the word of the Lord from Jerusalem. He shall judge between the nations, and shall rebuke many people; they shall beat their swords into plowshares and their spears into pruning hooks; nation shall not lift up sword against nation, neither shall they learn war anymore.

Isaiah 2:2-4

The New Testament says that Jesus Christ is coming back to rule and reign on the earth. His Kingdom will usher in a time of peace. However, as we have seen, our planet will have to endure a terrible time of hardship and suffering before that occurs. The center stage of this great drama is to unfold on the Temple Mount. What then does this all mean?

What Does This Mean for Israel?

The coming world events mean a terrible time of suffering for Israel. The person responsbile for this will be the false Messiah. Most of what we know about the origin, career and destiny of this false Messiah, we know from the Old Testament.[1] He will be the one who ushers in a time of persecution of Israel that will even eclipse the holocaust in Europe in the 30's and 40's.

The Old Testament refers to this period as the "Time of Jacob's Trouble" (Jeremiah 30:7).

Fortunately, an alert and informed few—a "remnant"—will recognize him for what he really is and will do their best to flee his influence. But this will require enduring great hardship since he will control the economic, political and religious systems of the world.

It will be the return of Jesus Christ Himself that will put an end to his reign, and the chaos he brings. It is at this time that God will complete His destiny for Israel by establishing the rule of the true Messiah on the throne of David and fulfilling the promises in Isaiah 2:2-4.

What Does This Mean for the Christian?

First of all, it is a reminder that God is not finished with Israel. One of the greatest problems that has plagued the church, has been the denial of the unconditional promises that God has given Israel. God is not through with Israel: Paul spent three chapters in his letter to the Romans—chapter 9, 10, 11—to make that quite clear.

The notion that these promises were forfeited when Israel rejected the Messiah has often led to anti-semitic abuse. The misconception that the promises given Israel have been transfered to the church has led to a misunderstanding of God's purposes for Israel. This misunderstanding will help set the stage for the next holocaust that Jesus predicted.[2]

What Should Christians Do About the Temple?

Christians are confronted with some important questions as to their involvement with the rebuilding of the Temple. What should a Christian do and not do?

There are Christians who feel compelled to become directly involved in the building of the Third Temple. The President of the Jerusalem Temple Foundation, wrote the following in a letter to Temple Mount supporters:

> I am sure that you are abundantly aware of the momentousness of the days in which we are living. Portions of the Holy Scripture that have been apocolyptic [sic] for centuries are being opened to us with amazing rapidity and regularity. We are seeing and experiencing the fulfillment of Biblical prophecy as time seemingly rushes before us with anticipatory and adventurous haste.
>
> . . . According to the Holy Scriptures, Gentiles or strangers were involved in the erection of the First

Temple in Jerusalem (2 Chronicles 2:17,18). It also seems apparent that strangers who came to Israel for the sake of the name of the Lord, were to be privileged to have the Temple as a focal point of prayer and worship (1 Kings 8.41-43). Because of these points and other pertinent scriptures, the Jerusalem Temple Foundation, U.S.A., has been established by Bible-believing Christians to make the church aware of its mandated responsibilities related to Israel, and in particular the Temple Mount and the preparation for the construction of the Third Temple on Mt. Moriah.[3]

On the other hand, there are Christians who see involvement in the Temple planning as a bad thing. Dr. Wesley Brown, who has spent a great part of his life living in Jerusalem, expressed his thoughts about Christians who support Temple Mount activists:

From my understanding of Scripture, they are supporting evil, he says. It's all very well for them to sit in America with their little prophetic charts, in their comfort, thousands of miles away, while we who live in Jerusalem will have to bury the dead when the kind of violence they are supporting actually comes to pass.[4]

Another periodical had this to say:

Christian Zionism is inherent in any literal interpretation of the Old Testament prophecies; those prophecies were to, for, and about Israel. When Christians interpret the Old Testament literally and fail to avail themselves of New Testament understandings of Old Testament prophecy and apocalypse, they become Judaized and philo-Semites [Christian Zionists]. Christians in general, however, need to be concerned about the phenomenon because it has dangerous potentials and because it represents heresy so far as doctrine is concerned.

As to the dangers: if the radical Christian Right were to succeed in taking over the Temple Mount, it would prompt Islam to embark upon a "holy war." Second, latent anti-Semitism could emerge when prophecy, for some reason, is interpreted in a way that disinherits Israel.[5]

Should the Christian leave this whole matter of the Temple Mount alone?

Though we know from the New Testament that a Third Temple is predicted and will be built, Christians should not participate in its planning, promotion or construction. This is not our cause.

Gentile participation in the building of the First Temple does not serve as a precedent for Gentile participation today. Those involved in building the First Temple were not Gentile believers. Their involvement was not due to their devotion to the God of Israel rather their services were conscripted. Therefore to assert modern day Gentiles should help with the rebuilding of the Temple finds no Biblical basis.

Built in Unbelief

Though the New Testament teaches that a Third Temple will be built, it also declares it will be built in unbelief of Jesus as the Messiah. The Third Temple will be the center stage for activities of the man of sin, the Antichrist. The future events surrounding the Third Temple will not honor Jesus in any way.

For the Christian there is no more need for a Temple. Jesus said about Himself, "something greater than the Temple is here" (Matthew 12:6).

When Christ died for the sins of the world He made possible, direct access to God the Father. The Bible says:

> For there is one God and one Mediator between God and men, the Man Christ Jesus (1 Timothy 2:5).

The need for a Temple and the sacrificial system is now gone, for they were fulfilled in the person of Jesus Christ. Those Christians who participate in the rebuilding efforts of the Third Temple would be sharing this unbelief.

The motives of some "to hasten the coming of the Lord" is equally a wrong motive. For one thing, God is running this universe according to His schedule, not man's. Furthermore those Christians who want the Temple built should realize that this will lead Israel into their worst Holocaust ever. There is no moral or Biblical justification in becoming involved in the building of the Third Temple. It is a Jewish cause.

Legitimate Causes

There are, however, legitimate causes concerning the Temple with which a Christian can involve himself. For one, the search for the location of the Temple. Such a matter has tremendous historical and archaeological value. Though Protestantism rejects the idea of "holy sites" or "shrines," the Temple Mount has great historical value. If surveyed, and eventually excavated, who knows what great finds might be there?

The freedom of worship issue is another matter in which Christians can get involved. The Temple Mount should be opened up to Moslem, Jew and Christian for free worship. What better place to proclaim to the world what is ahead for the future. The Temple Mount, itself, is the very place where many of the prophetic events will occur.

One of the possible solutions to the freedom of worship issue is the Temple Mount could be internationalized. Each of the three major religions, Judaism, Christianity and Islam have different weekly holy days on which they worship. For the Moslems it's Friday; the Jews, Saturday; and the Christians, Sunday. Each could have exclusive access to the Mount on their holy day.

Each believer needs to evaluate in their own heart their extent of involvement toward the Temple Mount with the Scripture as their guide.

The Ultimate Issue

These discussions quickly raise many prophetic issues that go far beyond the space we have available here. Indeed, it clearly is a time for us all to do our homework. It is time to find out what the Bible really says about the future.

The real issue is not the Temple. The ultimate issue is Jesus Christ Himself.

Was He really Whom He claimed to be? Is He really going to return as He said He would?

Our eternal destiny is determined by our relationship with Him. He is, after all, the ultimate issue.

Don't gamble your eternity hoping that the Bible is wrong! Investigate the claims of Christ. Take advantage of His completed work on your behalf. He has prepared an eternal destiny for you that is available for the asking.

If you were to die today, do you know for sure that you would be with Him in heaven?

If you would like to know more, contact the authors at the following addresses:

Don Stewart   Chuck Missler
Box 6486   Box 881
Orange, Calif. 92613   Big Bear Lake, Ca 92315

Endnotes

1. See our discussion in Appendix 6.

2. See Hal Lindsey, *Road to Holocaust*, Bantam Books, New York, 1989.

3. Charles Monroe, personal letter from the Jerusalem Temple Foundation, United States Headquarters, 11726 San Vicente Blvd. Los Angeles, California.

4. Haim Shapiro, Jerusalem *Post*, International Edition, July 2-8, 1984, p. 12.

5. Dr. O. Kelly Ingram, *The Link*, November, 1983, p. 9.

APPENDIX 1

THE BIBLICAL CASE FOR A THIRD TEMPLE

Does the Bible predict that a Third Temple is going to be built in Jerusalem? There is some controversy among Christian commentators as to whether the Bible teaches that a Third Temple or "tribulation Temple" will be constructed. We will briefly cover some of the main areas of this controversy.

Understand Prophecy Literally

The crucial issue boils down to how we interpret prophecy. There are two basic ways to interpret Bible prophecy. Either you understand it literally or you do not.[1] If a person rejects the literal interpretation then they are left to their own imagination as to what the Scripture means. We believe that a literal interpretation is the first option for anyone looking at Scripture. Someone has once said, "If the literal sense makes good sense, seek no other sense, lest you come up with nonsense."

We believe it makes sense to understand the Scriptures as literally requiring the eventual construction and desecration of a Third Temple.

Prophecy Literally Fulfilled

We also believe in the literal interpretation of the Bible because past prophecies have been literally fulfilled. An example is the return of Israel to its land. After the Second Temple was destroyed and the nation of Israel was scattered, Bible commentators tended to spiritualize the prophecies concerning Israel and the Temple.

About one hundred years ago William Blackstone wrote a book entitled *Jesus is Coming.* Blackstone took literally what the Bible said about the Second Coming of Christ. Hence he stated that Israel, though scattered for some 1800 years at that time, must return as a functioning nation again in their land. Though he was ridiculed for his interpretation, he proved to be correct.

Against all odds, the modern state of Israel was reborn on May 14, 1948. The rebirth of the nation Israel serves as a constant reminder of the faithfulness of God as well as an example that we should understand the Bible literally.

BIBLICAL EVIDENCE

The Bible, in both testaments, speaks of a Temple that has yet to appear.

Old Testament

There are three passages in the Old Testament that speak of the defiling of a future Temple. None of them have been literally fulfilled:

> Then he shall confirm a covenant with many for one week; but in the middle of the week he shall bring an end to sacrifice and offering. And on the wing of abominations shall be one who makes desolate, even until the consummation, which is determined, is poured out on the desolate (Daniel 9:27).

> And forces shall be mustered by him, and they shall defile the sanctuary fortress; then they shall take away the daily sacrifices, and place there the abomination of desolation (Daniel 11:31).

> And from the time that the daily sacrifice is taken away, and the abomination of desolation is set up, there shall be one thousand two hundred and ninety days (Daniel 12:11).

Jesus spoke of this prophecy being still future to His time (Matthew 24:15).

Isaiah

The prophet Isaiah may have been speaking of the Third Temple when he recorded God saying:

> Thus says the Lord: "Heaven is My throne and the earth is My footstool. Where is the house that you will build Me? And where is the place of My rest? For all those things My hands have made, and all those things exist," says the Lord. "But on this one will I look: on Him who is poor and of a contrite spirit, and who trembles at My word. He who kills a bull is as if he slays a man; he who

sacrifices a lamb as if he breaks a dog's neck; he who offers a grain offering, as if he offers swine's blood; he who burns incense, as if he blesses an idol. Just as they have chosen their own ways, and their soul delights in their abominations, so will I choose their delusions, and bring fears on them; because when I called, no one answered, when I spoke they did not hear; but they did evil before My eyes, and chose that in which I do not delight" (Isaiah 66:1-4).

New Testament

There are passages in the New Testament that require a rebuilt Temple in Jerusalem.

Abomination of Desolation

Jesus spoke of the Temple being desolated:

Therefore when you see the Abomination of Desolation which was spoken of through Daniel the prophet, standing in the holy place (let the reader understand), then let those who are in Judea flee to the mountains; let him who is on the housetop not go down to get the things out that are in his house; and let him who is in the field not turn back to get his cloak. But woe to those who are with child and to those who nurse babies in those days! But pray that your flight may not be in winter, or on a Sabbath; for there will be great tribulation, such as has not occurred since the beginning of the world until now, nor ever shall. And unless those days had been cut short, no life would have been saved; but for the sake of the elect those days shall be cut short (Matthew 24:15-22).

This is an event that has not yet happened though many have attempted to find some historical fulfillment.

Man of Sin

The Apostle Paul also spoke of the desolation of the Temple:

Let no one deceive you by any means; for that Day will not come unless the falling away comes first, and the man of sin is revealed, the son of perdition, who opposes and exalts himself above all that is called God or that is worshiped, so that he sits as God in the temple of God, showing himself that he is God (2 Thessalonians 2:3,4).

The English translation of "Temple"[2] in verse four is unfortunate. It is not the generic word for Temple ιερον (hieron) which refers to the Temple and its buildings. It is the Greek word ναος (naos) the "Sanctuary," the Holy of Holies. It is the most Holy Place that this individual sits:

This event, like the Abomination of Desolation, has not yet occurred.

Book of Revelation

The existence of a future Temple is confirmed by the John the evangelist in the Book of Revelation:

> Then I was given a reed like a measuring rod. And the angel stood, saying, "Rise and measure the temple of God, the altar and those who worship there. But leave out the court which is outside the temple, and do not measure it, for it has been given to the Gentiles. And they will tread the holy city under foot for forty-two months" (Revelation 11:1,2).

This is an important reference. John wrote the Book of Revelation approximately A.D. 90, *after* the Second Temple had been destroyed. He envisions the Third Temple existing during the time immediately *before* Christ comes back to earth.

These passages in Scripture show the need for a future Temple to fulfill all that the prophets have spoken.

NO THIRD TEMPLE?

Those who reject the idea that the Bible predicts that a Third Temple will be built do so for the following reasons:

No Future for Israel

There has been a tendency by many interpreters of Scripture to transfer the prophecies originally given to Israel to the New Testament church. According to this view the literal nation Israel does not have a special future in the plan of God. The prophecies that were originally given to Israel will now be fulfilled in the New Testament church. This view suffers from several problems:

1. The critical promises given to Israel were unconditional. There was no provision for forfeiture.

2. God is not finished with Israel. Paul allots three chapters in his letter to the Romans—9, 10 and 11–to deal with this very point.

3. God makes it clear that His regathering of Israel is for His reputation, not their worthiness (Ezekiel 36:21-24).

4. Jesus' briefing to the disciples is clearly to the Jews and not the church (pray that your flight be not on the Sabbath day etc.).

Prophecy Already Fulfilled

Many commentators believe the prophecy was already fulfilled. The abomination of desolation, they contend, was fulfilled at, or a few years before, the destruction of the Second Temple in A.D. 70. Others make it some other time in the history of the church.[3]

We believe all these interpretations fall short of what the Bible clearly says on the subject.

MISCELLANEOUS ISSUES

If the Bible does speak of a "tribulation Temple" that is yet to be built then a few questions naturally arise:

How Soon Can the Third Temple Be Built?

Once work on a Third Temple begins how long will it take before it can be completed? Dr. Asher Kaufman has suggested that, if given the opportunity, he could easily justify ten years of archaeological work on the Temple Mount to precede any actual building.

However, when a window of opportunity opens, it is surprising how quickly things can happen. The Berlin Wall is an excellent example.

The building itself could also be undertaken creatively since even Solomon's Temple was tooled elsewhere and moved into place. With the intensity of commitment and the creative resources of Israel, nothing should surprise us.

The Bible does not give a precise timetable as to when the Temple will be built. Since the Bible does not specifically say we can only speculate. The only thing for certain is that it does exist in the middle of the seven year period, the start of the Great Tribulation.

The Fate of the Temple

What will become of this tribulation Temple? It will probably be destroyed sometime during the Great Tribulation, possibly during a huge earthquake:

> In the same hour there was a great earthquake, and a tenth of the city fell. In the earthquake seven thousand men were killed, and the rest were afraid and gave glory to the God of heaven (Revelation 11:13).

Conclusion

From our brief look at Scripture we find that a rebuilt Temple is necessary to complete the plan of God. Though many Bible students do not believe the prophecies concerning the Temple are to be understood literally, it seems much more consistent to do so.

Endnotes

1.   Of course we understand that the Bible contains figures of speech. Literal interpretation allows for it and expects it. This has been dealt with elsewhere (Don Stewart, *What Everyone Needs to Know About the Bible*, Orange, California, Dart Press, 1992).

2.   Dr. Robert L. Thomas writes: "The man of lawlessness will occupy the holy precincts in order to accept and demand worship that is due God alone. This evidently is a Jewish temple to be rebuilt in Jerusalem in the future. Dependence of these words on Daniel 9:26,27;11:31,36,37;12:11 (cf. Matt. 24:15; Mark 13:14) demands such a reference. There is no impressive evidence for understanding naon ("temple") in a nonliteral sense.

   "Figurative meanings of ναos (naos, "temple") elsewhere, including its reference to the church . . . and possible allusions to the heavenly temple where God is . . . fall short of the literal significance required by the present passage. A human being can take his seat in none of these others. The article with naon (accusative) is a further indication that the Jerusalem temple of God is intended" (Robert L. Thomas in "The Expositors Bible Commentary," Vol 11. *Ephesians to Philemon*, Grand Rapids, Zondervan, 1978, pp. 322, 323).

   F. F. Bruce writes of the phrase, "taking his seat in the temple of God: " . . . the picture here is of a material shrine . . . The material temple in Jerusalem has much to be said in its favor." F.F. Bruce, *1 & 2 Thessalonians*, Word Bible Commentary, Waco, Texas, Word, 1982, pp. 168,169).

3.   For example, the fall of Jerusalem to Islam in the A.D. 638.

APPENDIX 2

A CHRONOLOGY OF IMPORTANT EVENTS CONCERNING JERUSALEM AND THE TEMPLE MOUNT

The Temple Mount and the city of Jerusalem have a central place in the history of Israel. The following are some of the most important events that have occurred to the city and the sacred Mount.

OLD TESTAMENT EVENTS   (BC)

2000 Abraham meets Melchizidek, King of Salem and Priest of "God most high" (El Elyon) Genesis 14:18-20, Hebrews 6:20-7:22). Abraham journeys three days from Beersheba or Gerar to Mt. Moriah in Jerusalem to offer his son Isaac as a sacrifice in obedience to God's command. God provides a ram as a substitute (Genesis 22, Hebrews 11:8-19).

1400 After setting up the Ark at Shiloh near Shechem, Joshua launches into Jerusalem (Joshua 10:23).

1000 The Jebusite stronghold in Jerusalem is captured by King David. The city of David is built south of the Temple Mount. David reigns thirty-three years in Jerusalem after a seven year reign in Hebron (2 Samuel 5:1-15). The Ark of the Covenant is returned by David into Jerusalem and placed in the Tabernacle Moses built there (2 Samuel 6:1-18); 1 Chronicles 15:1-16,43. David plans to build the First Temple but is not permitted because he is a man of war. He purchases Araunah's threshing floor and erects an altar of sacrifice on Mt. Moriah. This is the site of the First Temple.

950   Solomon with the help of Hiram of Tyre and 183, 600 workers builds the First Temple and royal palace. He uses local limestone, cedar from Lebanon and great amounts of gold and silver (1 Kings 5:9; 2 Chronicles 2). Solomon also enlarges the city (1 Kings 7:1-12). Building takes seven years.

935   The Kingdom is divided into North (Israel) and South (Judah). Ten Tribes are part of the Northern Kingdom while only two (Judah and Benjamin) belong to the southern.

910   Temple is plundered by Shishak (Sheshonk) Pharaoh of Egypt. Much gold and silver are taken (1 Kings 14:25-28; 2 Chronicles 12:1-11).

835   Joash repairs the Temple, establishes maintenance fund, and brings period of revival and reform to the southern kingdom (2 Kings 12:5ff).

720   Ahaz king of Judah dismantles Solomon's bronze vessels and places private Syrian altar in the Temple (2 Kings 16:1-20; 2 Chronicles 29-31). He later stripped the gold to pay tribute to Sennacherib.

716   Hezekiah, king of Jerusalem, with help of God, resists Assyrians attempt to capture Jerusalem (2 Chronicles 32). Wells and springs are stopped up.

640   King Josiah repairs the Temple and brings about national religious reforms (2 Chronicles 34,35). Last mention of the Ark of the Covenant.

606   Nebuchadnezzar lays siege to Jerusalem. He takes captives to Babylon including Daniel and his three friends.

598   Jerusalem is plundered by Nebuchadnezzar for a second time.

586   Nebuchadnezzar burns the city, and destroys the Temple. He murders many of the inhabitants and carries off a great number into captivity (2 Kings 24,25; 2 Chronicles 36).

573   Prophet Jeremiah predict a seventy year captivity in Babylon. The prophet Ezekiel, a captive in Babylon, receives a vision from God giving great detail of a future Temple that is to be built.

539   Belshazzar desecrates the Temple vessels in Babylon. Handwriting on the wall seals his fate that night as Babylon is taken by the Medes and Persians (Daniel 5).

538 Edict of Cyrus (Ezra 1:1).

536 The seventy years of captivity are over. Cyrus the Persian gives the decree as the prophet Isaiah had predicted 170 years earlier.

531 The first Jews return to Jerusalem from Babylonian captivity. They rebuild the walls and the city.

520 Beginning of rebuilding of Temple and return of Zerubbabel (Haggai 1:14,15).

515 Through the leadership of Nehemiah and Zerubbabel, the Second Temple is completed despite fierce opposition and delays. An altar of sacrifice is built on the Temple Mount. Temple is completed after a fifteen year delay (Ezra 6:15).

458 Ezra goes up to Jerusalem (Ezra 7:7,8).

445 Nehemiah arrives in Jerusalem (Nehemiah 2).

443 Walls are completed and restored. Nehemiah returns to the Persian court (Nehemiah 13:6).

432 Nehemiah returns to Jerusalem.

332 Flavius Josephus records that Alexander the Great's invading army is met by priests outside of Jerusalem. They convince him not to destroy Jerusalem by showing prophecy contained in Scripture concerning him. Alexander spares city and the Temple.

320 Jerusalem is captured by Ptolemy Soter.

314 The city is taken by Antiochus the Great.

301 Jerusalem is captured by Ptolemy Epiphanes.

170 Jerusalem is captured by Antiochus Epiphanes. Antiochus murders Jews and plunders Jerusalem. He offers a pig on the altar and carries off the Temple treasuries. Worship and sacrifice is halted.

166 Judas Maccabaeus leads a Jewish revolt that gains back Jerusalem. Temple is cleansed and sacrifices are restored (1 Maccabees 4).

164 Jerusalem is besieged by Antiochus Eupator.

141   The Roman fortress is conquered by the Maccabees freeing the Temple from pagan supervision.

126   Jerusalem is besieged by Antiochus Soter.

65   Jerusalem is besieged by Aratus.

63   Jerusalem is captured by the Roman general Pompey. Pompey enters the holy of holies in the Temple and is disappointed to find it empty.

40   Jerusalem is captured by the Parthians.

38   Taken by Herod the Great a cruel ruler who was a ruthless murderer. It was he who ordered the slaughter of the innocents at Bethlehem (Matt. 2). Herod ordered the Temple enlarged. A new Temple is rebuilt over the sight of Zerubbabel's Temple. Temple and courts rebuilt until A.D. 63. City and walls under construction for 46 years (John 2).

New Testament Events (6 B.C. to A.D. 60).

Luke 2   Jesus was circumcised and dedicated in the Temple.

Luke 2   At age twelve Jesus confounds the elders with His wisdom.

Matt. 4   At Jesus' temptation, the Devil takes Him to the pinnacle of the Temple.

John 2   Jesus cleanses the Temple.

Matt. 24   Jesus pronounces judgment on the Temple.

Acts 3   Peter and John heal a lame man at the gate beautiful.

Acts 12   Herod puts James to the sword.

AD

40   Roman Emperor Caligula orders an image of himself to be placed in the Holy of Holies. Order is not carried out and Caligula soon dies.

70   Roman General Titus lays siege to Jerusalem destroying inhabitants, city, and Temple. The Temple is set afire.

132-135   Bar Kochba rebellion. Jerusalem is in the hands of the Jews for three years. It is possible they started to rebuild the Temple.

135   The city is sacked by Hadrian after the Bar Kochba revolt. Aelia Capitolina is built over the rubble of Jerusalem.

333   Pilgrim of Bordeaux visits Jerusalem.

362   Attempt is made to rebuild the Temple.

614   Jerusalem is taken by the Persians.

629   Jerusalem is captured by Heraclius.

637   Captured by the Saracens under Omar ibn al-Khatab. Dome of the Rock completed.

715   Al Aqsa Mosque is completed.

1076   Atsiz takes Jerusalem from the Caliph al-Mostanther Billah.

1095   al-Afdhal ibn Bedr captures the city for Egypt after a 40 day siege.

1099   The Crusaders, under Godfrey de Bouillon, capture Jerusalem.

1187   Captured by Salah-ed-Din the great Moslem conqueror.

1244   Jerusalem is sacked by the Mongol Hordes.

1517   Selim I takes the city bringing it into the Ottoman Empire.

1822   Taken by Ibrahim Pasha of Egypt.

1917   Captured by General Allenby of Britain. He humbly walks into the city of Jerusalem.

1948   War between newly established Israel against Jordan and Egypt in Jerusalem after which part of the city remains under Israeli rule and part under Jordan.

Recent Events

The following is a more detailed chronology since the Old City of Jerusalem was regained by the Jews in 1967.

1967

June 7th   The Old City of Jerusalem falls into Israeli hands. Israeli paratrooper commander Mordehai Gur, mounted on a half track, takes the Temple Mount on the third day of the Six Day War. The Temple Mount is regained but authority is turned back over to the Moslems.

June 28   Prime Minister Levi Eshkol meets Moslem and Christian leaders from both side of the pre-war border and pledges free access to all holy places and the government's intention to place the internal administration for the holy places in the hands of the respective religious leaders. The same day the barriers came down between east and west Jerusalem.

August 1   Jerusalem police take on the maintenance of public order at the holy places in the Old City at the request of Moslem and Christian authorities who claim of improper behavior by visitors at the Church of the Holy Sepulchre and the Temple Mount.

August 8   A committee headed by the ministry of religious affairs Zerah Warhaftig is given cabinet responsibility for the Holy places in Jerusalem and the West Bank.

August 15   IDF Chief Chaplain Aluf Shlomo Goren, and fifty followers including other army chaplains hold a service on the Temple Mount. Goren contends that some parts of the compound are not part of the Temple Mount and therefore the ban against Jews stepping on the Mount until the Temple is rebuilt does not apply. He said his measurements were based upon Josephus, Maimonides, Sa'adia Gaon and archaeological evidence. He also declared that the Dome of the Rock is not the site of the Holy of Holies.The defense ministry criticizes Goren noting that he is a senior army officer. Goren claims he first met with Warhaftig and that the Moslem authorities consented to his prayers.

August 17   An Israeli Defense Forces spokesman reveals that the arms cache was found during the fighting in the Al Aksa Mosque.

August 22   The Chief Rabbinate puts up signs outside the Compound noting the religious ban on visiting the Temple Mount area.

Sept. 9   Moslems protest against the abolition of fees to enter the Temple Mount area. The Defense Ministry says that the Waqf can only charge fees to enter the Mosques.

1968

July 15   The President of the Moslem Court of Appeals turns down a request by an American Masonic Temple Order who asked permission to build a $100 Million "Solomon's" temple on the Temple Mount.

Dec. 19   Hanukka prayers are offered by a group of nationalistic Jews on the Temple Mount.

1969

April 15   State Attorney Zvi Bar Niv responding to an order against the Police Minister Shlomo Hillel, explains that Jews should not be allowed to pray on the Temple Mount because "premature prayer" by Jews on the Temple Mount would raise grave security and international political problems. The plaintiff is the Faithful of the Temple Mount.

August 21   A fire at the Al Aqsa Mosque guts the southeastern wing. Brigades from West and East Jerusalem fight the blaze together for four hours while an angry Moslem crowd chants "Allah Akbar" and "Down with Israel." A curfew is imposed on the Old City. The president of the Moslem Council claims arson and charges deliberately slow response on the part of the fire brigades. Arab states blame Israel.

August 23   A non-Jewish Australian tourist, Dennis Michael Rohan, identifying himself as a member of the "Church of God" is arrested as a suspect in the arson. East Jerusalem and major West Bank towns go on general strike as an expression of grief and sorrow over the fire. Police use force to break up a demonstration at the compound exit. Angry demonstrations break out in Arab capitals.

August 27   Rohan tells the court he acted as the Lord's emissary" in accordance with the Book of Zechariah. The Temple Mount is closed to non-Moslems for two months.

Dec. 30   Court convicts Rohan but declares him not criminally liable by reason of insanity.

1970

Sept. 9   High Court of Justice decides it has no jurisdiction in matters connected with the right and claims of different religious groups. Therefore it won't interfere with the position of the government prohibiting Jewish prayer on the Mount.

1971

March 11   Altercation on Temple Mount occurs when students led by Gershon Salomon,—a leader of the Faithful of the Temple Mount—try to hold prayers on the site.

1973

August 8   Despite police warnings, Rabbi Louis Rabinowitz and Knesset Member Binyamin Halevi pray on the Mount. They are removed.

October   The Yom Kippur War. Israel is attacked by four nations. Israel gains territory in the Sinai and Golan Heights. Temple Mount is not affected.

1976

Jan. 30   Magistrate Court Judge Ruth Or rules that Jews are permitted to pray on the Temple Mount. She acquits eight youths who were accused of disturbing public order by holding prayers on the site against police orders. Police Minister Shlomo Hillel says he will continue to bar prayers.

Feb. 1   Yitzhak Raphael, Minister of Religious Affairs, says praying on the Temple Mount is a religious law question and not in his jurisdiction.

Feb. 9   East Jerusalem high schools protest the court decision. The protests continue nearly two week with over 100 arrests. Shopkeepers strike and riots occur in West Bank towns. Security services impose inter-city travel ban.

Feb. 11   The January Magistrate Court decision of January 30th is appealed.

March 4   Kurt Waldheim, ex-Nazi and UN Secretary General, pledges to take up Islamic complaints about Israel interference with Moslem holy places and worshippers in Jerusalem.

March 8   A group of young people—many non-religious—led by Rabinowitz and Salomon are barred from the Temple Mount by police. The police say they are acting in accordance with the High Court decision of September 9, 1970 decision.

March 11   Ramallah Birzeit and El Bireh councils join Nablus in resigning to protest against police action against Arab demonstrations protesting Judge Ruth Or's Temple Mount decision.

March 17   Magistrate Or's ruling is overturned by Jerusalem District Court. The Court rules that eight Betar youths who attempted to pray "demonstratively" on the Temple Mount were guilty of behavior "likely to cause a breach of the peace." The court also rules that Jews have an "unquestionable historical and legal right to pray on the Temple Mount, but that these rights could not be exercised until the authorities had adopted regulations fixing the time and place for such prayers. Such regulations were necessary, said the court, in order to maintain public order. The court notes that the Religious Affairs Ministry had "good reason" for not yet setting the rules.

Aug. 10   The attorney general appeals to the Supreme Court on its Temple Mount ruling. Religious Affairs Minister Yitzhak Raphael will not rule on district Court jurisdiction until there's a Supreme Court decision.

1977

June 28   Interior Minister Joseph Burg, given the police is a part of his purview, notes that those trying to pray on the Mount are "not exactly from the God-fearing sector." He states "the law will be kept. That is taken to mean that the Jews would continue to be barred from attempting to pray on the Temple Mount on the coming Tisha B'Av.

August 14   (Tisha B'Av) An attempt by 30 members of the El Har Hashem (To the Mount of God) to pray on the Temple Mount is foiled by the General Security Services. At a press conference, the group led by Gershon Salomon, emphasizes the ties of the Jewish people to the site and claims it is "absurd" that Jews were forbidden from entering the compound.

1979

March 25   Rumors that followers of Meir Kahane and Yeshiva students would attempt Temple Mount prayers cause a general West Bank strike and bring 2,000 Arab youths with staves and rocks to the compound. They disperse after police intervention.

August 3   Land of Israel movement "Banai" and other nationalists, are prevented from praying on the Temple Mount.

1980

August 6   The High Court is asked to revoke ban on prayer on the Temple Mount, in light of clause three of the new Jerusalem Law, which guarantees freedom of access.

August 10   300 members of Gush Emunim try to force their way onto the Temple Mount and are dispersed by police.

1981

August 28   Religious Affairs Ministry workers are found digging a tunnel under the Temple Mount. The work began secretly a month earlier when water began leaking from a cistern under the Temple Mount and had to be drained. Chief Rabbi Shlomo Goren closes the dig because of the issue's sensitivity.

August 30   Former Deputy Prime Minister Yigael Yadin protests quasi-archaeological activities of Religious Affairs Ministry north of the Western Wall.

Sept 2   Jews and Arabs clash with stones and fists in a tunnel north of the Western Wall. The Arabs had attempted to seal the cistern. A group of Yeshiva students under orders from Rabbi Getz, rabbi of the Western Wall, knocked down the wall. The two groups were separated by police after a scuffle. Police inspector-General Arye Ivtzan says the cistern will be sealed to restore the previous situation—until there is a legal ruling. Ivtzan is praised by Mayor Teddy Kollek, and condemned by Goren, who says the cistern was part of the Second Temple and had nothing to do with Islam. The next day the cistern is sealed. Goren is quoted as saying the cistern was a tunnel that could lead to temple treasures "including the lost ark."

Sept. 4   A strike by the Supreme Moslem Council closes shops and schools in East Jerusalem to "protest against excavation under the Temple Mount."

Sept. 10.   The Waqf seals the cistern from the other side to prevent Jewish penetration. Meanwhile archaeologist Dan

Bahat discounts theories the cistern was connected with the Temple.

Sept. 15   Attempt by the Temple Mount Faithful to pray in compound thwarted by Moslem opposition. The High Court decides that the right of the Jew to pray on the Mount is a political issue upon which the government must decide. The Jerusalem Law doesn't cover the issue, rules the court.

1982

April 11   Israeli soldier Alan Harry Goodman, a U.S. immigrant goes on a shooting rampage on the Temple Mount. He kills one and wounds three. The incident sets off a week of rioting in Jerusalem, the West Bank, and Gaza and angry reaction internationally against Israel. At his trial Goodman told the court that by "liberating the spot holy to the Jews," he expected to become King of the Jews. A year after the incident Goodman is convicted and sentenced to life plus two terms of 20 years.

July 25   Yoel Lerner, member of Meir Kahane's Kach Party, is arrested for planning to sabotage one of the mosques on the Temple Mount.

Oct. 26   Lerner convicted of planning to blow up the Dome of the Rock . Previously he had served a three year sentence for heading a group that plotted to overthrow the government and establish a state based upon religious law. He was sentenced to two and one half years in prison.

Dec. 9   Knesset Member Geula Cohen charges that the Arabs have arm caches on the Mount.

1983

March 10   Police arrest more than forty people suspected of planning to penetrate the Temple Mount. Police had found four armed youths trying to break into the underground passage known as Solomon's Stables. Working on the basis of intelligence reports, the police surround the home of Rabbi Yisrael Ariél, former head of the Yamit Yeshiva. There, the others are arrested and a search of his apartment and others reveals several weapons and diagrams of the Temple Mount.

May 11   High Court allows Faithful of the Temple Mount to hold prayers at the Mograbi Gate on Jerusalem Day, after police had earlier denied them a licence. A similar decision is handed down for Tiasha B'Av.

May 22   SRI's seven man team was thwarted from performing the first scientific study of the Rabbinical Tunnel. Moslems called the Israeli police to stop scientific expedition.

Sept. 17   On Yom Kippur the police try to prevent former chief Rabbi Shlomo Goren from holding prayers in a room beneath the Temple Mount. Goren claimed he had the consent of IDF chief of staff Rav-Aluf Moshe Levy. Levy showed up for the prayers. Police then allowed the prayer to take place.

Sept 21   The Temple Mount 29 are acquitted of all charges against them. The police are reprimanded by District Court Judge Ya'acov Bazak and describes the 29 as "amateurish" But he does not rule on the legality of prayer on the Mount.

1990

Oct. 8   On Jerusalem Day, Temple Mount Faithful unfurls banner on Temple Mount. A riot breaks out leaving over twenty Palestinians dead. United Nations censures Israel for this act but says nothing as to those who started the riot. Press erroneously report that group was about to lay a foundation stone on the Temple Mount.

APPENDIX 3

THE WEALTH OF THE TEMPLE

In the past there have been those who have sought after the great treasures that were contained in the tabernacle in the wilderness and the two Temples in Jerusalem.[1] The Bible provides many examples of people who have plundered the wealth of the Temple. This fascination has continued in modern times for many of the excavations done in and around the Temple were nothing but treasure hunts. Because the Temple Mount in Jerusalem contains many subterranean chambers which are now filled with debris, there are those that wonder if some of the Temple treasures could have been hidden beneath the rocks in ancient times to escape plundering invaders.[2] This section will address this issue.

Egyptian Spoils

When the Jews made their Exodus from Egypt they took along with them gold, silver and various ornaments (Exodus 12:35). Part of this booty was used to construct the tabernacle which was built by the free will offerings of the people. The materials assembled for the tabernacle are described in detail in Exodus 35-38 and summarized in Exodus 38:21-30. The entire quantity collected of gold, silver and bronze were enormous. One ton of gold, 3 3/4 tons of silver and 2 1/2 tons of bronze! At today's prices for gold and silver the tabernacle, constructed by Moses, would have a value of over 15 million dollars.

From the Tabernacle to the Temple

We know that most, if not all of the holy vessels of gold and silver from the tabernacle were with the Ark of the Covenant when it was brought from the City of David to the First Temple built by Solomon (1 Kings 8:4).

It was David who made the plans and amassed the material for the Temple (1 Chronicles 28:1-19; 2 Chronicles 2-4; 1 Kings 6-7). These materials included 100,000 talents of gold and 1,000,000 talents of silver (1

Chronicles 29). David, from his own private fortune, gave 3,000 talents of gold and 7,000 talents of high grade silver. By anyone's standard this is an enormous quantity of gold and silver.

In addition to the gold and silver, great quantities of bronze, cedar iron, and precious stones were contributed. The most holy place of Solomon's Temple was lined with cedar from Lebanon and covered with 600 talents of gold. The doors of the Temple were also covered with gold plates.

During this period of Israel's history Solomon's yearly income was 666 talents of gold. At Solomon's time silver was as common as stone in Jerusalem (1 Kings 10:27). Solomon made 200 massive shields each weighing 300 shekels to hang on the walls of his palace. He also had an ivory throne overlaid with gold. Thus it is easy to see that "King Solomon surpassed all the kings of the earth in riches and wisdom" (1 Kings 10:23).

This splendor brought him recognition and fame throughout the world (1 Kings 10; 2 Chronicles 9).

Not Unreasonable Amount

In their commentary on the Old Testament Keil and Delitzsch call attention to the large quantities of gold and silver taken in Asia by Alexander the Great: 2,600 talents of gold and 600 talents of silver from Damascus, 50,000 talents of gold and 40,000 talents of uncoined gold and silver from Susa and from Persopolis 120,000 talents of gold. Thus, though the biblical accounts are very high, they are not unreasonable compared to the wealth of other surrounding ancient kingdoms.

The Plundering of the Temple

The tremendous wealth of the first Temple was plundered immediately after Solomon's death. This occurred during the reign of Rehoboam, the son of of Solomon. Shishak, the King of Egypt, sieged Jerusalem and "took away treasures of the house of the Lord and the treasures of the King's house." Shishak took away everything including 500 shields of gold which Solomon had made (2 Chronicles 12:1-12).

Second Chronicles 12 says that Shishak's army numbered 60,000 horsemen and 1,200 chariots. If each man carried back 100 pounds of booty, this would make only 3,000 tons of gold and silver. However the people with him were "without number," the "Lubim, the Sukkim, and the Ethiopians." These people may also have carried off the gold and silver. The Bible also indicates that that Shishak did not get all of the gold and silver for the golden lampstand; the Menorah, and the Ark of the Covenant were not taken.[3]

The Wealth Deteriorates

Israel began to deteriorate in strength after the death of Solomon. There were occasional revivals up until the Babylonian captivity where the populace made generous contributions to the repairs and refurbishing of the Temple. With the exception of these revivals the wealth of the Temple deteriorated due to the confiscation of the Temple funds to pay national expenses and tributes to foreign powers.

More Plundering

The Temple treasures were depleted by King Asa who sent all of the remaining gold and silver to the Syrian king Ben-hadad. This was an effort to buy the Syrians help against Baasha, the king of Israel (1 Kings 15:18,19).

Another plundering took place during the reign of Ahaziah when Jehoash, king of Israel carried off to Samaria "all" the gold and silver in the Temple and the palace (2 Kings 14:14). A further pilfering occurred when Ahaz took the palace and Temple treasures to secure the aid of the king of Assyria. Furthermore he removed the brazen altar from its site along with the bases and ornaments of the lavers (2 Kings 16:10-17).

Hezekiah

Later King Hezekiah would pay tribute to Sennacherib, king of Assyria, 300 talents of silver and 30 talents of gold:

> So Hezekiah gave him all the silver that was found in the house of the Lord and in the treasures of the king's house. At that time Hezekiah stripped the gold from the doors of the Temple of the Lord and from the pillars which Hezekiah king of Judah has overlaid, and gave it to the king of Assyria (2 Kings 18:15,16).

Later Hezekiah foolishly received the emissaries of the king of Babylon and showed them his remaining state treasures:

Hezekiah . . . showed them all the house of his treasures—the silver and gold, the spices and precious ointment, and all his armory—all that was found among his treasures. There was nothing in his house or in all his dominion that Hezekiah did not show them (2 Kings 20:13).

The wealth of the Temple at the time of Hezekiah was evidently more than enough to incite the covetousness of the King of Babylon so that he hastened to capture Jerusalem after his emissaries brought him the news of the great wealth there.

The Fall of Jerusalem

The fall of Jerusalem in 586 B.C. was accompanied by terrible destruction and much loss of life,

And all the articles from the house of God, great and small, the treasures of the house of the Lord, and the treasures of the king and of his leaders, all these he (Nebuchadnezzar) took to Babylon. Then they burned the house of God, broke down the wall of Jerusalem, and burned all its palaces with fire, and destroyed all its precious possessions (2 Chronicles 36:18,19).

A parallel account in 2 Kings 25 describes the seized vessels of the house of the Lord as including posts, snuffers, dishes for incense, firepans, bowls, etc.

Return from Exile

At the end of the seventy year captivity in Babylon, the returning Jews were allowed to carry back at least some of these gold and silver sacred objects to Jerusalem (Ezra 1:5-10). The list of returned items included 1,000 basins of gold, 1,000 basins of silver, 29 censers, 30 bowls of gold, 2,410 bowls of silver, and other vessels of gold and silver totaling 5469.

Those that returned from exile set about rebuilding the Temple and the walls. The Second Temple, completed in 515 B.C., was modest compared to that of Solomon. Nevertheless, the Second Temple contained large quantities of gold and silver which appears to have increased during the life of the Temple.

The Maccabees

The next plundering of the Temple took place during the time of the Maccabees. It was done by Antiochus IV Epiphanes in 167 B.C. and is described in 1 Maccabees 1:20 ff. and by Flavius Josephus. At that time the Temple contained at least an altar of incense of gold, the table of showbread, the lampstands, many cups, bowls, and incense holders, crowns and gold plating at the wall where the cherubim had been in days of old. Antiochus also took the "hidden treasures" of the Temple site. In three days' he murdered 40,000 Jews and took an equally number of captives. He then desecrated the Temple by sacrificing a pig on the altar.

Herod

The total wealth of the Second Temple was always small compared to the greatness of the First Temple. King Herod decided to completely rebuild and enlarge the second Temple beginning in the 18th year of his reign (ca. 20 B.C.). Herod employed 10,000 workmen and 1,000 wagons. The size of the Temple area was increased from 17 to 34 acres by excavations in the north and by the building of the great retaining walls rising 450 feet from the Kidron Valley in the southeast. The buildings and walls he built were extensive and massive.

The Temple treasury benefited by a great influx of gold and silver contributed by worshippers from all lands. Cicero wrote of great influxes of gold brought to Jerusalem during his lifetime. Gifts other than gold or silver were sold and their value given to the treasury. Another large source of revenue was profit made from the sale of the meat offerings which were prepared by the Levites and sold every day to the offerers. By far the largest sum was derived from the half-shekel of Temple tribute which was required of every male Israelite of age, including proselytes and slaves. The total sum of gold and silver contributed annually at the time of Jesus has been estimated to have been on the order of one half million dollars per year. A large fraction of this wealth no doubt accumulated year after year over the lifetime of the temples (515 B.C. to A.D. 70). There were numerous Temple expenses but the evidence suggests the bulk of the income was stored up year after year.

The Romans

Thus when the Romans plundered the Temple in A.D. 70 there take could have been worth tens of millions of dollars. The destruction was devastating for both the city and Temple were destroyed. Tradition has it that the intense flames melted the gold and silver so that it ran between the cracks of the rocks. Roman soldiers then totally dismantled the Temple, stone by stone, to extract the gold. This fulfilled a prophecy given by Jesus who predicted that the Temple would be destroyed and not one stone would be left on top of one another (Matthew 24:1,2). No one knows if any of the vessels or sacred objects from Herod's Temple were hidden in subterranean passageways during the long siege of Titus. Most everything of value was no doubt carried off to Rome.

Conclusion

The overall impression from all the biblical accounts and from tradition is that the various plunderings of Jerusalem's temples were always thorough and total. While no gold or silver may be buried underneath the Temple Mount, objects of priceless archaeological, historical, and religious significance may lie there.

Endnotes

1.   The authors are indebted to Lambert Dolphin for much of the content of this chapter.

2.   Found among the Dead Sea Scrolls was the Copper Scroll which speaks of the hidden treasures of the Temple. Acccording to this scroll the hidden gold and silver would equal about 200 tons. This has caused many to conclude that the story is fanciful. The scroll also provides directions and clues to locate the treasure. Unfortunately, the clues are so obscure that no one has been able to decipher them.

APPENDIX 4

THE MOST AMAZING PROPHECY IN THE BIBLE—DANIEL 9

The most amazing passage in the Bible clearly establishes, to any reasonable, rational person, the Bible's supernatural origin from outside the domain of time itself. It demonstrates its uniqueness by describing, in exquisite detail, key events before they happen.

It is the realization of this uniqueness that causes major changes in a person's entire outlook—in fact, changes ones entire life.

It is important to know, first of all, that Daniel is part of the Old Testament, and thus was translated into Greek almost three centuries before Christ was born. This is a well established fact of secular history.[1]

The Septuagint Translation

The famous conqueror Alexander the Great promoted the Greek language throughout the known world, and thus virtually everyone in those days spoke Greek. Even among the Jews, Hebrew fell into disuse, being reserved primarily for ceremonial purposes. (Somewhat analogous to the former use of Latin among the Catholics).

In order to make the Tanach, (what Christians call the Old Testament) available to the average Jewish believer, a project was undertaken to translate the Hebrew scriptures into Greek. Seventy scholars were commissioned to complete this work and the result is known as the Septuagint ("70") translation of the Old Testament. It is abbreviated as LXX.

It is critical to our interest to establish that the book of Daniel was, thus, in documented form almost three centuries before Christ was born.[2]

Daniel was deported as a teen-ager to be a slave in Babylon along with his people. This captivity was to last 70 years. Near the end of this period, the angel Gabriel appeared to Daniel and gave him a four verse prophecy

that is unquestionably the most remarkable passage in
the entire Bible. (Daniel 9:24-27)
These four verses include the following:

9:24   The scope of the prophecy: 70 weeks (of years)
9:25   The events of the first 69 weeks of years
9:26   The events during a interval between the 69th and
        70th week of years;
9:27   The "Seventieth Week" of years (yet future)

Seventy weeks ("sevens") are determined for your
people and for your holy city, to finish the transgression,
and to make an end of sins, and to make reconciliation for
iniquity, and to bring in everlasting righteousness, and to
seal up vision and prophecy, and to anoint the Most Holy
(Daniel 9:24).

The idiom of a week of years was common in Israel as a
"sabbath for the land" in which the land was to lie fallow
every seventh year. Their failure to obey these laws led to
their captivity by the Babylonians.[3]
The focus of the passage is upon "your people and upon
your holy city": that is, upon Israel and Jerusalem; not the
world in general.
The scope of this prophecy is conspicuously broad and
the final "week" of years is yet future and is known among
Bible scholars as the "Seventieth Week" of Daniel. (Most of
the book of Revelation in the New Testament appears to be
an elaboration of the events of this seven-year period).
The fascinating prediction occurs in verse 25.

Know therefore and understand, that from (1) the
going forth of the commandment to restore and build
Jerusalem (2) unto the "Messiah the Prince" there shall
be seven weeks, and threescore and two weeks: the street
shall be built again, and the wall, even in troublesome
times.

This is a mathematical prophecy and we are indebted
to Sir Robert Anderson, former head of Scotland Yard,
whose famous book, *The Coming Prince*, details the
analysis behind this passage.[4]
The commandment to restore and build Jerusalem was
given by Artaxerxes Longimanus on March 14, 445 B.C.
(The emphasis on the street and the wall being rebuilt is to
avoid confusion with other mandates involving the Temple
rather than the city itself.)

"The Messiah the Prince" is actually the "Meschiach Nagid" in the Hebrew (מָשִׁיחַ נָגִיד): "The Messiah the King." (Nagid is a word meaning king[5]; the English translation as "Prince" is unfortunate).

It is fascinating to note that during the ministry of Jesus Christ, there were several occasions in which the people attempted to promote Him as their King, but He carefully avoided it.[6] "Mine hour is not yet come," was His response.

Then one day, He meticulously arranged it.[7] On this particular day He rode into the city of Jerusalem on a donkey, deliberately fulfilling a prophecy by Zechariah that the Messiah would present Himself in just that way.[8]

This is the only occasion that Jesus presented himself as King. This occurred, according to Sir Robert Anderson's dating, on April 6, A.D. 32. [9]

The Jewish (and Babylonian) calendars used a 360 day year, and 69 weeks of years totals 173,880 days. The angel Gabriel, in effect, told Daniel that the interval between the commandment to rebuild the city of Jerusalem until the presentation of the Messiah as King would be 173,880 days. When we examine the period between March 14, 445 B.C. and April 6, A.D. 32, and correct for leap years, etc., we discover that it is 173,880 days exactly, to the very day![10]

How could Daniel have known that in advance? How could anyone have contrived to have that prediction documented over three centuries in advance?

But there's more.

> And after the sixty- two weeks Messiah shall be cut off, but not for Himself: and the people of the prince who is to come shall destroy the city and the sanctuary. The end of it shall be with a flood, and till the end of the war desolations are determined (Daniel 9:26).

The "threescore and two weeks" follow the initial seven weeks, so verse 26 deals with events after the 69th week. The Messiah is to be "cut-off": the Hebrew word is כרת (karat) which means to be executed for a capital crime. That is exactly what happened at the crucifixion.

Subsequently, "the people of the prince that shall come" (another leader we discuss in Appendix 6) would destroy the city and the sanctuary. The very week that Jesus presented himself, he also predicted the destruction of Jerusalem:

For the days will come upon you, when your enemies will build an embankment around you, surround you and close you in on every side, and level you, and your children within you, to the ground; and they will not leave in you one stone upon another because you did not know the time of your visitation (Luke 19:43,44).

Thirty eight years after Christ was crucified, Titus Vespasian, with the Fifth, Twelfth, and Fifteenth Roman Legions leveled the city of Jerusalem in A.D. 70 , exactly as both Daniel and Jesus had predicted in advance.

It is provocative to recognize that Luke 19:44 indicates that Jesus held them accountable to have recognized this day from Daniel's prophecy!

This unique prediction totally defies any human explanation.

Numerous books have been written detailing the incredible predictions of the Bible and are worthy of careful study. The conspicuous result is simply that the track record of the Bible is unique and unequalled in the records of human history.

And it raises a very critical issue. Was Jesus the Christ—Yeshua HaMaschiah—really Whom He claimed to be? Was He really the voice of the "burning bush" Who spoke to Moses? Was He the incarnate Creator Himself?

He is scheduled to return to the earth to rule as its king? If so, what are the implications for you and me?

They are more significant than any other discovery we will ever make.

Endnotes

1. Encyclopedia Britannica, Vol. 14, p. 762; Vol 22, p. 413, etc.

2. The Book of Daniel is actually one of the best authenticated books of the Old Testament, but this approach is a convenient short-cut for our purposes here.

3. II Chronicles 36:20,21: And them that had escaped from the sword carried he away to Babylon; where they were servants to him and his sons until the reign of the kingdom of Persia: To fulfil the word of the LORD by the mouth of Jeremiah, until the land had enjoyed her sabbaths: for as long as she lay desolate she kept sabbath, to fulfil threescore and ten years.

4. The classic work in this area of prophecy is one that we strongly recommend: Anderson, Robert, K.C.B.,LL.D., *The Coming Prince,* London: Hodder & Stoughton, 1894. Also, Grand Rapids, Michigan: Kregel Publications, 1954.

5. First used of Saul, the first king of Israel.

6. John 6:15: When Jesus therefore perceived that they would come and take Him by force, to make Him a king, He departed again into a mountain Himself alone. He was always in control: John 7:30,44; 8:59; 10:39.

7. Luke 19:28-40.

8. Zech 9:9: Rejoice greatly, O daughter of Zion; shout, O daughter of Jerusalem: behold, thy King cometh unto thee: he is just, and having salvation; lowly, and riding upon an ass, and upon a colt the foal of an ass.

9. Harold Hoehner places the command of Artaxrexes on March 5, 444 B.C. He dates the crucifixion on March 30 of A.D. 33.

10.   Gabriel's prophecy in Daniel Chapter 9:

‘69 weeks x 7 years/week x 360 days/year =
173,880 days

Anderson's analysis of actual history:

445 B.C. - A.D. 32 = 476 years
(remember, no Year 0)

476 years x 365 days/year = 173,740 days
March 14 - April 6 =   · 24 days
days for leap years =   116 days

total   173,880 days

Gabriel's Prophecy = 173,880 days
Approximation error = 0 days!

APPENDIX 5

EZEKIEL'S TEMPLE

When Jesus returns to the earth there will be a final Temple that will be built in Israel. The prophet Zechariah predicted in 500 B.C. that the Messiah will build a Temple in Israel.

Take the silver and gold, make an elaborate crown, and sit it on the head of Joshua the son of Jehozadak, the high priest. Then speak to him, saying, 'Thus says the Lord of hosts, saying: "Behold the Man whose name is BRANCH! From His place He shall branch out, and he shall build the temple of the Lord: Yes, He shall build the temple of the Lord. He shall bear the glory, and shall sit and rule on His throne; so he shall be a priest on His throne, and the counsel of peace shall be between them both (Zechariah 6:11-13).

This is the Temple that is seen in Ezekiel's vision (Ezekiel 40-45). It is commonly referred to as "Ezekiel's Temple" because of the detailed description given in the Book of Ezekiel. This Temple, according to Ezekiel 48, will evidently not be built at Jerusalem but at Shiloh. Shiloh is located 31 kilometers to the north of Jerusalem.

There are, however, some who believe that the Fourth Temple will be built over the same spot as the previous three.

Memorial

This Temple will be a memorial, a center to teach people about God's holiness. It will remind them of the great sacrifice God made for mankind when Christ died on the cross.

The Fourth Temple evidently is established to teach invisible realities to those who are born and raised on earth during the millennium.

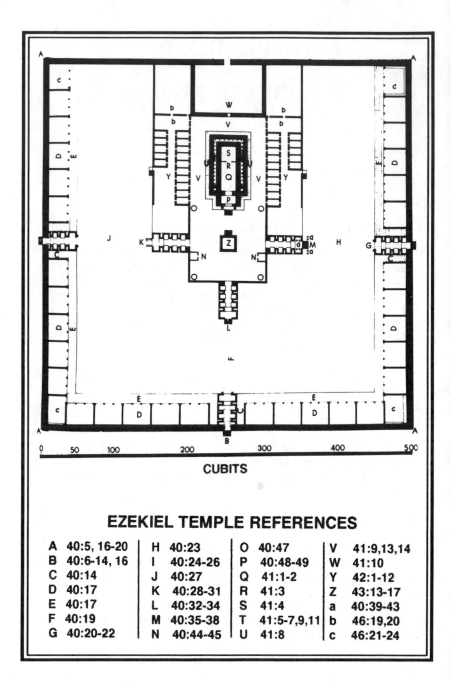

EZEKIEL TEMPLE REFERENCES

A	40:5, 16-20	H	40:23	O	40:47	V	41:9,13,14
B	40:6-14, 16	I	40:24-26	P	40:48-49	W	41:10
C	40:14	J	40:27	Q	41:1-2	Y	42:1-12
D	40:17	K	40:28-31	R	41:3	Z	43:13-17
E	40:17	L	40:32-34	S	41:4	a	40:39-43
F	40:19	M	40:35-38	T	41:5-7,9,11	b	46:19,20
G	40:20-22	N	40:44-45	U	41:8	c	46:21-24

Understood Literally?

Description of the Fourth Temple is so precise and detailed that it should be understood literally. While Ezekiel's account is explicitly detailed, many different conjectural models have been developed. One example is included (page 226).

There are several objections that are raised against a literal understanding of the Fourth Temple.

1. The death of Christ made the Old Testament sacrifices unnecessary.
2. The system was not to be restored for believers.
3. There is no future for Israel in God's program.

All Christians admit that the death of Christ brought an end to the need for sacrifices for our redemption. As the Old Testament sacrifices pointed forward to the work of Christ on the cross, these sacrifices will have value in looking back and remembering what He has done. As the Lord's supper is celebrated today as a memorial for the believer, so will the sacrificial system that will be administered in the future.

Although the Old Testament covenant was replaced by the new covenant (Jeremiah 31:31), it does not necessarily follow that the church age is the last of God's operations upon the earth.

The New Testament does not teach that the church is the new Israel. Usually people wish to take the promises associated with Israel and apply them to the church. Unfortunately, they do not seem as interested as applying the curses to Israel as well!

No Temple Needed in Eternity

After a one thousand year reign of Christ on the earth He will make a new heaven and a new earth. There will be no Temple in this new heaven and new earth:

> And I saw no Temple in it, for the Lord God, the Almighty, and the Lamb, are its Temple (Revelation 21:22,23).

The Lord God Himself will dwell with His people for all eternity. The historical Temples that were constructed will be only a memory.

APPENDIX 6

THE COMING WORLD LEADER

The coming world leader has about fifty titles in the Bible, but he is most often referred to as the "Antichrist" in Christian circles. Interestingly, most of what we know about his origin, role, career, and destiny, we learn from the Old Testament.

A complete discussion of this man of destiny far exceeds the space available here, but for those who would like to explore more, the following study outline is included. Many of the references are subtle and may require expositional commentary.

The authors intend to write a comprehensive book about this timely topic in the near future.

Titles

Old Testament

Adversary	Ps. 74:8-10; Isa. 59:19
	Lam 4:11, 12, Amos 3:11
Assyrian	Isa. 10:5,12
Belial	Nahum 1:15
Bloody and Deceitful Man	Ps. 5:6
Branch of the Terrible Ones	Isa. 25:5
Chief Prince	Ex. 38:2
Crooked Servant	Job 26:13
Cruel One	Jer 30:14
Destroyer of the Gentiles	Jer 4:7
Enemy	Ps. 55:3
Evil Man	Ps. 140:1
Head over many countries	Ps. 110:6
Head of the Northern Army	Joel 2:20
Idol Shepherd	Zech. 11:16,17
King of Princes	Hos. 8:10

King of Babylon	Isa. 14:11-20
Little Horn	Dan. 7:8-11,21-26;8:9-12, 23-25
Man of the Earth	Ps. 10:18
Merchant, with balances of deceit who loves to oppress	Hos 12:7
Mighty Man	Ps. 52:1
Nail	Is. 22:25
Prince that shall come	Dan. 9:26
Prince of Tyre	Ezek. 28:2-10
Profane Wicked Prince of Israel	Ezek. 21:25-27
Proud Man	Hab. 2:5
Rod of God's Anger	Isa. 10:5
Seed of the Serpent	Gen 3:15
Son of the Morning	Isa. 14:12
Spoiler, Destroyer	Isa. 16:4,5
Vile Person	Dan. 11:21
Violent Man	Psa. 140:1,10,11
Wicked, Wicked One	Psa. 9:17; 10:2,4; Is 11:4; Jer 30:14,23
Wilful King	Dan. 11:36

New Testament

Angel of the Bottomless Pit	Rev. 11:9
Antichrist, Pseudo Christ	1 John 2:22
Beast	Rev. 11:7
False prophet	Rev 13
Father of the lie	John 8:44; 2 Thess 2:11
Lawless One	2 Thess. 2:8
Man of Sin	2 Thess. 2:3
One who comes in his own name	John 5:43
Son of Perdition	2 Thess. 2:3
Star	Rev. 8:10
Unclean Spirit	Matt. 10:43
Vine of the earth	Rev. 14:18

The leader will be a Jew: Ezek. 21:25-27; Ezek. 28:2-10 (of the circumcision); Dan 11:36,37; John 5:43 (allos, not heteros: Jew, not a Gentile); Antichrist = "pseudo Christ": Received by Israel; Ps 55.

The leader will be the Son of Satan; Gen 3:15; Isa. 27:1; Ezek. 28:12-19; Rev. 13.

Some believe it is Judas Iscariot reincarnated: Ps 55:11-14; Matt. 12:41-43; John 17:12; John 6:7, 2 Thess. 2:3; Acts 1:25; with Rev. 11:7.

He will be an intellectual genius: Dan. 7:20; 8:23; Ezek 28:3.

He will be an oratorical genius: Dan 7:20; Rev 13:2.

He will be a political genius: Dan 11:21.

He will be a commercial genius: Dan 8:25; Rev 13:17; Ps. 52:7; Dan 11:38, 43; Ezek 28:4,5.

He will be a military genius: Dan 8:24; Rev.6:2; Rev 13:4; Isa 14:16.

He will be a governmental genius: Rev 13:1,2; 17:17.

He will be a religious genius: 2 Thess. 2:4 ("Allah"?); Rev 13:3 See also Ps 10, 52, 55 Isa. 10-14; Jer 49-51; Zech 5; Rev 18.

SELECTED BIBLIOGRAPY

Anderson, Sir Robert, *The Coming Prince*, Kregel Publications, Grand Rapids, Michigan, 1954.

Bahat, Dan, *Historical Atlas of Jerusalem*, Carta, Jerusalem, 1989.

Ben-Dov Meir, *In the Shadow of the Temple*, Harper and Row Publishers, New York, 1982.

DeHaan, M. R., *The Tabernacle*, Zondervan Publishing House, 1958.

Edersheim, Alfred, *The Temple, its Ministry and Services*, Wm. B. Eerdmans Publishing Co. Grand Rapids, MI, 1958.

Fletcher, Sir Bannister, *A History of Architecture*, Athlone, Press, London, 1975.

Hammond, Philip C., "New Light on the Nabateans," Biblical Archaeological Review, March/April 1981..

Jerome, *Commentary on Isaiah.*

Josephus, Flavius, *Antiquities of the Jews.*

Josephus, Flavius, *The Jewish War.*

Kaufman, Dr. Asher Selig, "The Temple of Jerusalem," *Tractate Middot*, Har Yera'eh Press, Jerusalem, 1991.

Kaufman, Dr. Asher Selig, "New Light Upon Zion, The Plan and Precise Location of the Second Temple," *Ariel*, Number 43, Jerusalem, 1977.

Kaufman, Dr. Asher Selig, "Where The Ancient Temple of Jerusalem Stood," Biblical Archeological Review, Vol IX No. 2, March/April 1983.

Kaufman, Dr. Asher Selig, *Christian News From Israel*, 1979.

Ledeen, Barbara and Michael, "The Temple Mount Plot," The New Republic, June 18, 1984.

Lindsey, Hal, *The Road To Holocaust*, New York, Bantam, 1989.

Mazar, Benjamin, *The Mountain of the Lord*, New York, Harper and Row, 1975.

Missler, Chuck, Commentary on the Old Testament, on tape cassettes, Koinonia House. Box 881, Big Bear Lake, Calif 92315

Missler, Chuck, Signs in the Heavens, Koinonia House. Box 881, Big Bear Lake, Calif 92315

Palestine Exploration Fund, Annuals and Quarterly
Reports

Patten, Donald W. Ronald R. Hatch, Loren C. Steinhauer, *The Long Day of Joshua and Six Other Catastrophes*, Baker Book House, Grand Rapids, Michigan, 1973.

Pragai, Michael, *Faith and Fulfillment*, 1985

Runciman, Steve, *A History of the Crusades*, Cambridge University Press, 1951

Spanier, Ehud (ed.) *The Royal Purple and the Biblical Blue*, Keter Publishing House Jerusalem Ltd., 1987. The Study of Chief Rabbi Dr. Isaac Herzog on the dye industries in ancient Israel and recent scientific contributions.

Steckoll, Solomon, *The Temple Mount*, Tom Stacey Ltd. London, 1972

Ward-Perkins, J. B., *Etruscan & Roman Architecture*, Penquin, Harmondsworth, 1970

Ward-Perkins, J. B., *Roman Architecture*, H. M. Abrams, New York, 1977

Ward-Perkins, J. B., *Roman Imperial Architecture*, Penguin, Harmondsworth, New York, 1981

Yadin, Yigael, *The Temple Scroll*, Steinmatskys, Tel Aviv, 1985

General References

Encyclopedia Britannica

Encyclopedia Judaica

About the Authors

ABOUT THE AUTHORS

Don Stewart

Don Stewart is one of the most successful writers in the country having authored or co-authored over twenty books. These include the award winning *Family Handbook of Christian Knowledge: The Bible, You Be The Judge,* and *The Ten Wonders of the Bible.*

Don's writings have also achieved international success. Twenty-four of his titles have been translated into different languages including Chinese, Finnish, Polish, Spanish, German, and Portuguese.

Don received his undergraduate degree at Biola University majoring in Bible. He received a masters degree from Talbot Theological Seminary graduating with the highest honors. Don is a member of the national honor society, Kappa Tau Epsilon.

Don is also an internationally known apologist, a defender of the historic Christian faith. In his defense of Christianity he has traveled to over thirty countries speaking at colleges, universities, churches, seminars, and retreats. His topics include the evidence for Christianity, the identity of Jesus Christ, the challenge of the cults, and the relationship of the Bible and science.

Because of his international success as an author and speaker, Don's various books have generated sales of over one million copies.

Other Books By Don Stewart from Dart Press

You Be The Judge: Is Christianity True?

The Ten Wonders of The Bible

Basic Bible Study Series:

* What Everyone Needs To Know About **God**

* What Everyone Needs To Know About **Jesus**

* What Everyone Needs To Know About **The Holy Spirit**

* What Everyone Needs To Know About **The Bible**

To order books call toll free
1-800-637-5177

Books Coming From Don Stewart in 1992

In Search of the Lost Ark: The Quest for the Ark of the Covenant

Basic Bible Study Series:

* What The Bible Says About The Future

* What The Bible Says About Science

Chuck Missler

Chuck Missler is regarded as one of the best known Bible teachers in the world, and has over 6 million tape cassettes distributed in over thirty countries. He has taught the Monday night Bible Study at Calvary Chapel in Costa, Mesa California for the past 20 years.

Chuck has appeared on television on numerous occasions and has regularly scheduled radio programs throughout the United States.

As a high technology executive, Chuck has served on the Board of Directors of over a dozen public corporations engaged in various scientific fields and has served as Chief Executive Officer for six of them.

Chuck has been associated with the ministries of Hal Lindsey, Chuck Smith, the late Walter Martin, and others. He is a frequent conference speaker as well as a staff resource to a number of churches in Southern California. Chuck is also the Executive Editor of Countdown, a Christian Intelligence News Journal focusing on a Biblical perspective of current events.

Chuck is the author of *The Rise of Babylon and the Persian Gulf Crisis* (with Hal Lindsey).

Tape sets available from Chuck include:

The Coming Temple
Genesis and the Big Bang
The Flood of Noah
Signs in the Heavens
Monuments: Sacred or Profane
Footprints of the Messiah
The Seventy Weeks of Daniel

Chuck also has expositonal commentaries of the Bible on tape.

To contact Chuck write:

Koinonia House
Box 881
Big Bear Lake, California 92315